GOD'S WAY

DAY BY DAY

CHARLES F.
STANLEY

www.jcountryman.com
A division of Thomas Nelson, Inc.
www.thomasnelson.com

A Gift for:

_____

From:

_____

God's good and perfect gifts
flow from His goodness.

JANUARY

*You are God's
unique and special creation.*

YOUR DESTINY

I have come that they may have life,
and that they may have it more abundantly.
JOHN 10:10

God has a master plan for your life, and that plan does not change. It is a plan designed specifically for you. It is a plan that God intends for you to live out fully, beginning at the moment of your birth and continuing until the moment of your death. God's plan for you has a purpose, a blueprint for your particular life, a character-development plan, a communication plan, a call to service, a guidance plan, and a blessing plan. . . . Your destiny is to be the person God has created you to be.

DOES GOD CARE?

The Lord is near to all who call upon Him.
PSALM 145:18

God is involved with you every moment of your life. You cannot shut Him out or turn Him away. There is not a single moment or situation with which He is unfamiliar or uninvolved.

Does God care that you are in debt and money is in short supply?

Does God care that the air-conditioning in your car no longer works?

Does God care that your feelings were hurt in an argument that you had with your stepmother?

Yes!

WALKING IN WISDOM

*Do not be unwise, but understand
what the will of the Lord is.*
EPHESIANS 5:17

We must choose to pursue wisdom. It's up to each of us to determine how we will walk through this life. Wisdom is not something a person stumbles into or acquires automatically; it must be sought out and pursued.

The person who walks in wisdom is very aware of his life, how he affects the world, and how the world affects him. He recognizes that every person faces three enemies in life: the world system, the flesh, and the devil. He seeks to know God's plan and purpose—not only for his personal life but also for every situation involving other people around him.

ABIDING ASSURANCE

He who is in you is greater than he who is in the world.
1 JOHN 4:4

God's peace is not an escape from reality. We are not transfixed or somehow mentally "removed" from feeling pain or struggling. Peace is not a stupor that dulls our senses. It is not an elimination of responsibility for addressing hard issues and difficult circumstances. Rather, peace is an undergirding rock-solid foundation so that no matter the tears we cry or the sorrow we feel, deep down inside we know with an abiding assurance that God is with us. God is in control, and the joy of the Lord is going to emerge far greater than any depth of agony we may be experiencing.

THE HELPER

You shall receive power when
the Holy Spirit has come upon you.
ACTS 1:8

If there ever was a group who should have
been able to live a consistent Christian life by
just doing their best, it was the apostles. Think
of all their advantages. They had been trained
by the Master. They had seen lame men walk,
blind men see, and the dead rise. . . . They had
even performed miracles themselves! . . . Yet in
their last encounter with the Savior, He let them
know that they were still missing something. . . .

Jesus knew they were not yet ready for the
task to which they had been called. They would
need more than their human spirit to carry
them They would need more than sheer
determination to fulfill their task. . . . They
needed the Holy Spirit.

GIVE AND RECEIVE

Give, and it will be given to you.
LUKE 6:38

B e quick to serve others. In giving, you will receive.

There's an old but true phrase, "To make a friend, be a friend." To give acceptance to others is to receive acceptance. To widen your circle of friends to include others is to be included in the broader circles of their lives.

Jesus taught, "Give, and it will be given to you." When you give to others a sense of belonging, you feel a greater sense of belonging.

THE LORD'S WORK

Whatever you do, do it heartily,
as to the Lord and not to men.
COLOSSIANS 3:23

Paul defined the Lord's work as "whatever you do." Because we are servants of God, everything we do is considered part of that service. God makes no distinction between what is spiritual and what is secular. . . .

All of us who know the Lord—homemakers, bankers, mechanics, assembly line workers, construction workers—are involved in God's work. We are all a part of what He is doing. It takes just as much dependency on the Holy Spirit to do any of these jobs well as it does to preach a sermon or sing in the choir. In some cases, it takes much more.

COMPLETE IN CHRIST

You are complete in Him,
who is the head of all principality and power.
COLOSSIANS 2:10

In Christ, we are made ready, we are equipped, for any crisis or circumstance that may come. . . .

The children of Israel wandered in a wilderness, but their shoes didn't wear out, even though they wandered there for forty years. When the children of Israel needed water, God supplied it. When they needed food, He sent manna. When they needed guidance, He gave them a very clear and present witness to lead them by day and by night. When they were surrounded by enemies, He delivered them. His means were sovereign and supernatural, and His provision was complete and sure. We can trust the Lord to do the same for us.

QUIETNESS AND REST

Let the peace of God rule in your hearts.
COLOSSIANS 3:15

The Greek word for peace means to "bind together" something that has been broken or disjointed. I think this is a superb illustration for how alienated men and women—so often feeling empty and disconnected from each other and God—can find a way to unity and wholeness. God's peace comes to them when they are united by faith with God.

This Greek word also refers to a prevailing sense of quietness and rest in a person's heart and emotions—of being unperturbed and unruffled. Peace is synonymous with being tranquil, serene, untroubled, and calm. It is a very real "state" of the soul.

EVERYONE CAN BE WISE

Wisdom rests in the heart of him who has understanding.
PROVERBS 14:33

The good news about God's wisdom is this: Every person *can* become wise. That isn't true for fame, fortune, or education. Not all people have the intellectual ability to earn college degrees. Not all people have the talents or attributes that contribute to fame. Not all people have the skills and opportunities necessary for acquiring wealth.

But every person can reverence God, can receive Jesus Christ as Savior, and can submit his or her life to God on a daily basis. *Every* person can become wise.

TRUSTING GOD

*Keep my soul and deliver me; let me not be ashamed,
for I put my trust in You.*
PSALM 25:20

David did not go from being a favorite person in the king's court to being king. The Lord allowed David to be in exile for more than a decade, all the while refining certain leadership skills in him. In exile, David wrote many of the psalms that we have in our Bibles today. In exile, David learned to trust God in all circumstances, regardless of his personal feelings. Those years of being on the run from Saul, often fearful for his very life, were years that the Lord used to refine certain competencies in David—to make him an excellent statesman and military commander as well as a compassionate leader and provider for his followers.

ROOM TO GROW

Not that we are sufficient of ourselves to think of anything as being from ourselves, but our sufficiency is from God.
2 CORINTHIANS 3:5

Each of us will always have plenty of room for growth, and that's part of God's design for us. We also will never be fully adequate because we will always have a need for God to do in us, for us, and through us what He alone can do. God is the author and finisher of our lives; not only of our faith, but of all aspects of the potential He has built into us. . . .

Don't ever lock yourself into saying, "I can't, I can't, I can't," when you feel less than fully competent. Instead say, "By the grace of God and with the help of God, I can."

GOD'S WISDOM

The wisdom that is from above is first pure,
then peaceable, gentle, willing to yield, full of mercy and
good fruits, without partiality and without hypocrisy.
JAMES 3:17

God's wisdom produces behavior that is morally pure, chaste, and modest.

God's wisdom produces relationship, not estrangement.

God's wisdom does not demand its own way but rather functions by influence.

God's wisdom is not rooted in pride but rather in service.

God's wisdom is marked by kindness, generosity, and helpfulness.

STAND AT THE CROSS

You are a chosen generation,
a royal priesthood, . . . His own special people.
1 PETER 2:9

We do not acquire feelings of self-worth by standing in front of a mirror and repeating to ourselves, "I am worthy, I am worthy, I am worthy." We acquire feelings of self-worth when we stand in front of the cross and come to the realization of the greatest truth of all time, "I am worthy because God says I am worthy. I am worthy because Jesus died in my place for my sins so that I might live in eternity with God."

GOD LOVES YOU

*The love of God has been poured out in our hearts
by the Holy Spirit who was given to us.*
ROMANS 5:5

God loves *you*. He loves you unconditionally, without limit or qualification, and He loves you personally and individually.

Not only does He love you and desire to shower you with His love, but He desires to be loved by you.

Furthermore, He desires that you love and be loved by other human beings. God is generous—even extravagant—in His love. He delights when you express His brand of unconditional love to others and when you experience that kind of love in return.

FORGIVEN

*If indeed I have forgiven anything, I have
forgiven that one for your sakes in the presence of Christ.*

2 CORINTHIANS 2:10

If God has forgiven you, forgive others, forgive yourself, and then open yourself up to the good opportunities that God has for you.

True, you may still have to live with consequences related to the sin. But you are never required by God to live with guilt, shame, or regret. Accept that your past mistakes may have put you into the situation you are in, but quickly acknowledge the greater truth that your past mistakes—now forgiven by God—do not need to impact the decisions or choices you will make in the future.

BLESSINGS AND REWARDS

Great is the LORD, and greatly to be praised.
PSALM 48:1

God is the source of all truly good things. What the Father gives us is for our perfection. He does not play favorites. He does not hold out something to us and then snatch it back at the last minute. God does not play games with His blessings or His rewards.

God may withhold some things from us at a particular time or in a particular season of our lives in order to work out something in our characters or in our spiritual development, but ultimately everything our hearts truly desire is possible for us to experience and to attain.

VIRTUES OF THE SPIRIT

Those who receive abundance of grace and of the gift of righteousness will reign in life through the One, Jesus Christ.
ROMANS 5:17

The best picture of what a Spirit-filled person looks like is Christ. His life was characterized by love, joy, peace, patience, and so on in the midst of a world characterized by just the opposite of those things. He was certainly not weak. He stood up to his detractors when it was appropriate. But He knew when to keep silent as well. He had the courage and wit to take on the intellectuals of His day. He spoke with authority. . . . He was a very secure man. There was nothing pretentious or intimidating about Him. At the end of His life He tackled the toughest opponent of all—death. And He won!

GOD'S SURE PROMISES

He is the living God, and steadfast forever.
DANIEL 6:26

When we approach and claim the promises of God in the Bible, we do so on the basis that our position is in Christ. We do not claim the promises of God because we feel at one time that the promises are true for us or we feel positive in a particular situation that God is going to act on our behalf. We claim the promises of God as true for us because of what Jesus has done for us, what God has said He would do for us, and what the Holy Spirit is available to do in us, through us, and for us. Our access to the reality of God's promises is not based on anything that we are or have done; it is based on who God is, what Jesus Christ has done, and what the Holy Spirit desires to do.

UNLIMITED SPIRITUAL GROWTH

Your right hand has held me up,
Your gentleness has made me great.
PSALM 18:35

When you think of your potential, don't limit yourself to thinking of ways in which you might expand your personal resume to include more and greater accomplishments. Think in terms of spiritual depth. God has planned unlimited growth for you in your inner person. He has boundless love for you and, therefore, a fullness of relationship with Him that only a few will experience—not because God desires to limit His availability, presence, or power to only a few, but because only a few will commit themselves to knowing God in more spiritually intimate ways.

GODLY LIVING

His divine power has given to us all things that
pertain to life and godliness, through the knowledge of Him
who called us by glory and virtue.

2 PETER 1:3

Your heavenly Father has offered you the most amazing gift that you can ever receive— the gift of His Son and full forgiveness of your sin nature through believing in His Son. He is not going to withhold from you anything that will enable or assist you in taking Jesus into the world in which you live and work. God desires for you to display your relationship with Jesus in every facet of your life, and He will grant every request you make that furthers the witness of Christ Jesus in you and through you.

PROSPERING IN ALL THINGS

*Beloved, I pray that you may prosper in all things
and be in health, just as your soul prospers.*
3 JOHN 2

Does God bless those who love and serve Him and walk according to His ways? Absolutely. When you walk in wisdom, you will prosper.

God's prosperity is for the whole person—spirit, mind, and body. The Bible says, "Beloved, I pray that you may prosper in all things and be in health, just as your soul prospers" (3 John 2). That one verse encapsulates the totality of prosperity—prosperity in one's health, in one's soul, and in all things—which includes all relationships, endeavors, investments, and the management of all possessions.

GO TO GOD

The eyes of the LORD run to and fro throughout
the whole earth, to show Himself strong on behalf of those
whose heart is loyal to Him.

2 CHRONICLES 16:9

What should we do when anxiety strikes? First and foremost, we must ask God to give us His peace and His truth.

Very specifically, we must ask God to deal with the problems that are filling both our conscious and subconscious minds. This is not something we do just once. It is something we may have to do many times throughout the day.

We must ask the Lord to help us focus all of our thoughts and energy on the immediate situation at hand.

GOD KNOWS YOUR NEED

He shall cover you with His feathers,
and under His wings you shall take refuge.
PSALM 91:4

Do you believe that God is surprised by the need you are experiencing? Do you believe that your sudden lack in a certain area of your life is either a mystery or a surprise to God? To the contrary—God knows you far better than you will ever know yourself. He knew about this need in your life long before you were ever conceived in your mother's womb. Not only did God know about that need, but He knew His provision for meeting that need. Just as your need is no surprise and no mystery to Him, neither is the provision for solving your problem or meeting your need hidden from His understanding or ability.

CHARACTER THAT ENDURES

If we live in the Spirit, let us also walk in the Spirit.
GALATIANS 5:25

Just as unconditional love shines brightest in the midst of our differences, so the fruit of the Spirit demonstrates its divine source when circumstances and relationships take a turn for the worse. The reason is, the fruit of the Spirit is just that: *fruit produced by the Spirit.* It is not fragile. It is not subject to change. Its root is deeply embedded in the person of Christ. When we abide in Him and allow Him to live His life through us, the result is character that endures the challenges of life.

SIN AND TEMPTATION

Follow His steps: "Who committed no sin. . . ."
1 PETER 2:21–22

Is temptation a sin? No. It is not a sin to be tempted. Jesus was tempted and the Bible clearly states that He lived His life without sin or deceit (1 Pet. 2:22). Sin occurs when we yield to temptation. It is at the point where we give in to a temptation that we sin.

A thought popping into your mind is not a sin. Jesus had to think about what the devil said to Him in the wilderness; He had to deal with the tempting thoughts that the devil prompted. The thought of sin is not at all the same as an act of sin. It is when we act on tempting thoughts in a way that crosses the boundaries of God's commands that we enter into sin.

DO SOMETHING SPECIFIC

The LORD will guide you continually,
and satisfy your soul in drought.
ISAIAH 58:11

Many times God will reveal a plan for meeting your need, and that plan very often includes something specific that you must do.

A young man was discussing his love life— or rather, his lack of a love life—with his grandfather. He admitted to his grandfather that he hadn't been out on a date in several months. He finally gave a big sigh and said to his grandfather, "Gramps, I guess I'm just going to have to trust God to send me a wife."

His grandfather replied with a twinkle in his eye, "I suspect that God would be a lot more eager to help you if He knew you had the nerve to ask the girl He sends you out on a date."

AN ACT OF THE WILL

*In everything give thanks; for this is
the will of God in Christ Jesus for you.*
1 THESSALONIANS 5:18

When the car breaks down without warning or the children are sick or your husband loses his job or a good friend rejects you, your emotions are tender. You don't feel that your life is going the way it should. Most important, the Lord doesn't expect you to. Jesus knows what it's like to experience grief and heart pain so deep it tears at the fiber of your being. . . .

Thanksgiving is an act of the will. It means looking at a negative circumstance and acknowledging that God allowed it into your life for a reason. . . . You can thank Him in full faith because you know the current pain is an opportunity for Him to demonstrate His grace on your behalf.

GOODNESS AND KINDNESS

Love your enemies, bless those who curse you,
do good to those who hate you.
MATTHEW 5:44

The only possibility of turning an enemy into a friend is by showing kindness to that person. Enemies don't become friends by force or by acts of vengeance. Rather, our enemies become friends when we express the love of God to them, do good to them, speak well of them, and pray for them.

If you show kindness to an enemy, God will reward you. Even if your enemy continues to persecute you and do evil to you, God will find a way to bless you.

GUARDING YOURSELF

Be strong in the Lord and in the power of His might.
EPHESIANS 6:10

Ask for the Holy Spirit's help and guidance as you enter situations or encounters that you believe may produce temptation.

Guard against putting yourself in a personal circumstance in which your perception may be clouded. A word I recommend frequently is HALT:

H = Hunger. Never allow yourself to
      become too hungry.
A = Anger. Never allow yourself to
      become too angry.
L = Lonely. Never allow yourself to
      become too lonely.
T = Tired. Never allow yourself to
      become too tired.

JESUS IS TRUTH

"I am the way, the truth, and the life."
JOHN 14:6

When we become a friend of Jesus, something revolutionary happens inside us. Our spirits, our hearts, our souls, our perspectives on life, and our capacities to love all change dramatically. We become a "new creation." . . .

Jesus gives to us something far more valuable than any human friend can ever give: He reveals to us the truth about God . . . the truth about ourselves . . . the truth about the relationship He desires to have with us . . . and the truth He desires for us to have with other human beings. He reveals in His own presence within us the whole truth, and nothing but the truth. He is Truth.

FEBRUARY

*Those who fear God stand
in awe of Him.*

SOMEBODY SPECIAL

*Those who know Your name will put their trust in You; for You,
LORD, have not forsaken those who seek You.*

PSALM 9:10

God says that you are a special. You are so
special and valuable to Him that He sent
His Son, Jesus Christ, to die for your sins, and
He made it possible for the Holy Spirit to come
and dwell within you to remind you on a daily
basis that you are a somebody in His eyes. You
are valuable beyond measure to God!

EACH NEW DAY

Apply your heart to my knowledge
. . . so that your trust may be in the LORD.
PROVERBS 22:17, 19

How many times have you found yourself saying at the end of a day, "When I got up this morning, I certainly didn't think I was going to have to face that today"? Our daily lives tend to be a mixture of negative and positive surprises. Rarely can we anticipate all that will happen to us.

We need to have a fresh encounter with God's Word as we prepare ourselves to walk into each new day. And then, all through the day, we need to turn our minds back to what we have read in the Scripture.

BLESSINGS AND BENEFITS

Oh, taste and see that the LORD
is good; blessed is the man who trusts in Him!
PSALM 34:8

P art of the reason God allows us to
experience sorrow and trials in this life is so
we might learn that God has power to sustain
us and provide for us all things that produce
earthly blessings and eternal benefits. . . .

All of God's children go through storms in
their journeys through life. It is precisely in the
"going-through" stage of any crisis that God's
peace is most clearly manifested to all.

THE TEMPLE OF GOD

Do you not know that you are a temple of God,
and that the Spirit of God dwells in you?

1 CORINTHIANS 3:16

Having grown up a devout Jew, Paul had a great deal of respect for the temple. To the nation of Israel, it represented the presence of God among His people.

When Christ was crucified, there was no longer any need for the temple. God no longer needed a building. He was free to take up residency in the heart of man. . . .

By referring to believers as temples, Paul was announcing that God had changed His residency for good. He had left the temple in Jerusalem and, through the person of the Holy Spirit, had moved into the hearts of His people.

VALUED BY GOD

*We are His workmanship, created in Christ Jesus for good works,
which God prepared beforehand that we should walk in them.*
Ephesians 2:10

I have met a number of people through the
years who have been told from their childhood,
"You'll never amount to anything." What a
terrible message regarding a person's worthiness
or value.

The truth of God is what that person needs
to hear! God says you *do* amount to something.
You are so valuable that God desires to live with
you forever. He desires to transform your sin
nature into the very nature of Christ Jesus.
He has a plan and purpose for your life, and He
desires to help you fulfill that plan and purpose
by giving you the Holy Spirit.

LOVE AND DEVOTION

Having been justified by faith, we have
peace with God through our Lord Jesus Christ.
ROMANS 5:1

G od wants us to respond to Him out of love
and devotion. Our motivation in serving
others is to be solely because we love God, not
because we think we have to do certain good
works to please God. When you love a person,
you are quick to see what you can do to show
that person how much you love her or him.
That's far different from doing things for a
person so that the other person might approve
of you, like you, or love you. The same is true
for your relationship with God. He already loves
you, likes you, and approves of you. Nothing
you can do will change that. . . . There
shouldn't be anything that you feel you have to
do to win God's approval.

GOD RESCUES US

The LORD is my rock and my fortress and my deliverer.
PSALM 18:2

Bad things happen. Trouble appears at the most inopportune times. Disaster strikes. And we are left to face the consequences. . . .

We step blindly into a wasps' nest of trouble and find ourselves nursing painful wounds, trying to pull out the stingers and vowing never again to get hurt, only to find that we don't have the power to keep free from the dangers that cross our paths.

But often, sudden tragedy or personal loss can open us up to our need for help, comfort, and guidance. And it is at this very point of need that our kind and loving God can open the window to our hearts. When we give the okay, God will come to our rescue.

STANDING IN AWE

The fear of the LORD is the beginning of wisdom.
PROVERBS 9:10

"Fear" in this verse refers to reverence for God. Those who fear God stand in awe of God. They have at least a glimmer of understanding that God is omniscient (all-wise), omnipotent (all-powerful), omnipresent (present in every moment and throughout all eternity), and all-loving, and that they are not. They stand before God in wonderment and amazement that God, who is all, has all, and controls all, cares, loves, reaches out, and blesses the individual human being. To fear God is not to fear God's judgment; it is to stand in awe that God has all authority to judge and to forgive, to show mercy, and to grant His grace in overflowing abundance.

DEVELOP YOUR GIFTS

*There are many plans in a man's heart,
nevertheless the LORD's counsel—that will stand.*
PROVERBS 19:21

If you are not fully aware today of the unique talents and gifts that God has given to you—and that have been present in you from your birth—ask God to reveal those gifts to you.

Once God reveals your unique talents, ask Him to help you develop them. Be sensitive to ways in which you might receive further training in your area of talent. . . .

As you develop your talents, ask God to reveal ways in which you can use your talents for His glory. Don't wait until you are an expert. Part of the way to become an expert is to start using your talents for God's purposes.

BECOMING GOD'S BEST

Blessed be the God and Father of our Lord Jesus Christ,
who . . . has begotten us again to a living hope.
1 PETER 1:3

God desires that we develop in our talents, aptitudes, and ministry gifts every day of our lives. We should never stop practicing or stop learning, no matter how experienced and skilled we may become. I'm told that the truly great concert pianists still practice scales on a routine basis. Top athletes still work out and practice "basic drills" during training camps and warm-up sessions, no matter how many years they've been in the professional ranks. . . .

God will not lead you to "become" something without aiding you to become the "best" you can possibly be in that area. He will not give you a talent and then fail to give you opportunities for discovering, using, developing, practicing, and perfecting it.

KNOWING GOD

Wisdom is better than strength.
ECCLESIASTES 9:16

The person who is seeking to walk in wisdom is going to reflect often about his own relationship with the Lord and how the Lord desires to work in his life. He is going to want to please the Lord, to grow in his relationship with the Lord. . . .

As we walk in wisdom, we see God's hand at every turn. We know He is with us. We become more and more familiar with His voice . . . His prompting . . . His leading . . . His tug at our hearts. We don't merely know more about God—rather, we truly come to know God in a deeper and more intimate way.

GOD MEETS OUR NEEDS

The LORD raises those who are bowed down;
the LORD loves the righteous.
PSALM 146:8

God is aware of, concerned about, and involved in every area of need you have, great or small.

Too often, however, we want to face and deal with only our external needs. We want God to provide a quick answer for us only in the tangible, material realm of life. To dig deeper into our neediness is something we perceive as painful, unnecessary, or too spiritual. God doesn't agree with that approach. While He is concerned about the needs we face in the practical and natural realm of life, He is even more concerned about the needs that impact our very identity and our potential as human beings.

REMINDED OF TRUTH

The Holy Spirit . . . will teach you all things, and bring to your remembrance all things that I said to you.

JOHN 14:26

Part of what the Holy Spirit does in your life is to remind you of the truth you have learned. Part of His role is to give you an understanding of what you have learned— He imparts to you God's reasons and purposes, and reveals to you God's deepest meanings and desires.

The law tells you that you *have* to. The grace of God as manifest in the Holy Spirit gives you the *want* to.

The law tells you that you must obey. The Holy Spirit has been imparted to you by the Father to help you obey.

GOD FORGIVES

You, LORD, are good and ready to forgive,
and abundant in mercy to all those who call upon You.
PSALM 86:5

Remember always . . .
What God forgives, He forgives completely.
What God heals, He brings to wholeness.
What God restores, He does so without any limitations placed upon a person's potential for sharing the gospel and being a witness of God's love, mercy, and grace.

BEGIN AGAIN

Not by works of righteousness which we have done,
but according to His mercy He saved us.
TITUS 3:5

The only thing we can do when we realize that we have yielded to temptation, that we have sinned before God, . . . is to ask for God's forgiveness. No amount of self-justification will work. No amount of making amends or doing penance will compensate for our sin. We must come to God and humbly confess our sin, ask Him to forgive us and to free us from the guilt of our sin, and ask Him to help us not to sin again. And then we must begin again, determined that we will neither listen to Satan nor ponder the things that God has forbidden us to experience.

SPIRITUALLY MINDED

To be spiritually minded is life and peace.
ROMANS 8:6

Spirit-filled men and women are not isolated from what's going on around them. And they are not without their faults. They experience hurt and disappointment like everybody else. They have their daily bouts with temptation.

What sets them apart from the rest of the world is their response. When circumstances wreak havoc with the peace of Spirit-filled people, there will be some downtime. But they won't stay down. They refocus their attention on the big picture, acknowledge the truth that their peace is from the Lord, and then move on. . . . They know that "the mind set on the things of the Spirit is life and peace."

ABUNDANT LIFE

*Seek first the kingdom of God and His righteousness,
and all these things shall be added to you.*
MATTHEW 6:33

E very human being ever born has had one
need in common. This need is the most
basic one of life, and ultimately it is the only
essential need. It is the need to be forgiven of
one's sin nature and come into right relationship
with God so that one might experience an
abundant life now and in eternity hereafter.

One of the great truths is this: all other
needs are secondary to this need to be born
again spiritually. It is equally true that once this
need is met in a person's life, all other needs *can*
be met, and until this need is met, most other
needs *cannot* be met.

GOD'S GRACE

Let us therefore come boldly to the throne of grace, that we may obtain mercy and find grace to help in time of need.
HEBREWS 4:16

God's love and God's forgiveness go hand in hand. As do God's love and God's grace. When you accept God's grace, you rest in the knowledge that God is in control of your life. You aren't the one in control. What happens to you is ultimately of God's doing. He is responsible for the consequences and the fashioning of your life. As He leads you from person to person, task to task—to say and do and be His person on the earth—you have an abiding sense that you are fulfilling His purpose for your life. That is the greatest feeling of fulfillment you can know. Such is a life of great meaning and purpose.

ABIDING IN CHRIST

If you abide in Me, and My words abide in you,
you will ask what you desire, and it shall be done for you.
JOHN 15:7

To abide in Christ is to be in union with Christ. It is to dwell in Him completely, without any part of our being kept outside Him. We are entirely submissive to Christ and subject to His command over our lives. We do not choose to do anything without Him. In fact, we *can't* succeed at doing anything without Him. Christ lives in us and we live in Him. As we abide in Him and in His teaching, we make our requests and receive God's provision.

WALKING WISELY

The LORD gives wisdom; from
His mouth come knowledge and understanding.

PROVERBS 2:6

Those who have the Holy Spirit resident in their lives do not automatically make wise choices and engage in wise actions. Furthermore, it is one thing to know what to do and another thing to do it. We must consciously and intentionally ask the Holy Spirit to guide us into wisdom and give us the courage to walk in it. . . .

We continually find ourselves in new situations, facing new circumstances. To walk wisely, we must consciously and intentionally ask the Lord daily to reveal His wisdom in every area of challenge, difficulty, or opportunity we face.

CHOOSING TO TRUST

Do not fret—it only causes harm.
PSALM 37:8

Concern is productive. It is forward-looking and positive.

Anxiety is the opposite—it is counterproductive, stuck in the present, and negative.

Concern motivates us to take action. Anxiety paralyzes us.

Concern may very well be marked by tears, expressions of sorrow and sympathy, empathy, thoughtful reflection, and quiet time for meditation. In the end, however, concern leads us to make decisions. It leads us to the point of saying, "I choose to trust in God. I choose to seek His plan and purpose in this. I choose to take the action He leads me to take."

OUR GENEROUS GOD

Blessed be the LORD God, the God of Israel,
who only does wondrous things!

PSALM 72:18

God will not withhold anything from you that is rightfully yours as His child.

God will not hide any aspect of His character from you.

God will not deny you any promise that He makes in His Word.

God will not shut you away from any blessing that is for your eternal benefit or that is required for the fulfillment of your purpose on this earth.

And best of all, God has already prepared for you all that you will need for every day of the rest of your life.

OUR PROVIDER

Keep me as the apple of Your eye;
hide me under the shadow of Your wings.
PSALM 17:8

God will use various people and resources to provide for us. But HE is the source. Remembering that is the key to staying dependent. We have a tendency to confuse the gift with the giver. It is easy to get our eyes focused on the provision rather than the provider. When that happens, our loyalty and trust shift as well. We begin seeking things and people rather than God. Without realizing it, we become idolaters.

God is the source of everything you need. Your children, job, spouse, and friends are only tools He uses to meet the needs in your life. He, however, is the source.

SACRIFICIAL LOVE

I lay down My life. . . . No one takes it from Me.
JOHN 10:17–18

Jesus chose to die for us out of His infinite, unconditional love for us. His life was not taken from Him—He purposefully and willfully laid it down in order that you and I might have eternal fellowship with God.

Nobody else can love you as much as Jesus loved you in dying for you. A person may die on your behalf to save your life . . . but nobody else can ever die to save your eternal soul. No sacrifice that any other person makes can ever equal what Jesus has done on your behalf.

OUR TEACHER AND GUIDE

When He has come, He will
convict the world of sin, and of righteousness.
JOHN 16:8

Sometimes God's role is to instruct us in the way we should go. It is then our responsibility to do what He has told us to do.

At other times God's role in meeting our needs is to supply Himself. God the Holy Spirit has been given to those who believe in Jesus Christ to be our Comforter, Counselor, Spirit of truth, and Helper. Jesus used these words to describe the work of the Holy Spirit in us. Guidance, comfort, courage, insight, truth, discernment, wisdom, understanding, peacefulness, strength—all of these are imparted to us by the Holy Spirit to help us see clearly and then walk boldly in the path God puts before us.

FRIENDSHIP WITH THE FATHER

He will love you and bless you and multiply you.
DEUTERONOMY 7:13

The goal of the believer is not just to be a Christian but to cultivate an intimate, devoted relationship with the heavenly Father.

God wants you to know Him; to enjoy Him; to live continually in the light of His favor, wisdom, and truth. He desires a genuine relationship with you, His child. Daily worship and prayer are the spiritual closet where you and the Father are drawn into a personal intimacy. There, God's love for you and your love for Him become the bedrock of your faith.

THE GIFT OF FRIENDSHIP

Greater love has no one than this,
than to lay down one's life for his friends.
JOHN 15:13

Many people think of assets in terms of real estate, stocks and bonds, or material possessions. Some think in terms of natural talents or spiritual gifts.

The dearest treasure of your life—second only to your relationship with Jesus Christ—is a close friend.

A friend loves you unconditionally, catches you when you fall, believes in the best for you and encourages the best in you, understands your deepest concerns, applauds your successes and shares your pain, offers you constructive criticism in times of error, and feels sorrow for you in times of pain or rejection. A genuine friend is a gift of God's mercy to you.

FACING FEAR

The battle is the LORD's.
1 SAMUEL 17:47

David *ran* toward Goliath. He ran in *faith* based upon God's previous deliverance of him from a bear and lion. He ran in *confidence*, knowing God had given him the ability to both run fast and use a sling well. He ran with *wisdom*, knowing he had chosen exactly the right stones.

As you look back over your life, you no doubt can recount many instances in which God has been with you in fearful circumstances. He has delivered you before. He has given you certain abilities and strengths. He promises in His Word to impart wisdom to you if you will only ask. At times you need to confront a frightening situation in a very direct and practical way. Run toward that thing that is causing fear, trusting God even as you go.

MARCH

*Jesus is the
cornerstone of our peace.*

BALANCED AND GROWING

*Cause me to know the way in which
I should walk, for I lift up my soul to You.*
PSALM 143:8

If a three-legged stool has one leg that is longer or shorter than the others, the stool is out of balance. It is unstable. God's desire for you is that you be emotionally stable, consistent, reliable, and even in your temperament. He desires for your physical needs to be satisfied. He desires for your spiritual life to be balanced and growing. His will is never for one of His children to be on an emotional, physical, or spiritual roller coaster of extreme highs and lows. Rather, He desires that you be in balance and that you be able to confront both positive and negative situations with a consistency of joy, love, and peace.

DIGGING INTO GOD'S WORD

*This Book of the Law shall not depart from
your mouth, but you shall meditate in it day and night.*
JOSHUA 1:8

To meditate on God's Word requires first that we read it. You can't think all day about something you haven't read!

To meditate means to dig into the deeper meaning of what God is saying in His Word. We aren't just to skim the Bible's pages, limit ourselves to our favorite verses or passages, or read at the surface level. We are to read the whole of God's Word so we can avail ourselves of the whole of God's truth. We are to read slowly, intently, looking for new insights.

PEACE WITH GOD

My peace I give to you; not as the world gives.
JOHN 14:27

What the world offers as "peace" is ultimately an illusion, even though it may appear very concrete. It is like a mirage in the desert. A mirage looks like a body of water. But in fact, it does not exist and therefore is never attainable. A mirage has absolutely no ability to quench thirst.

The world regards peace as being the by-product of doing the right deeds, saying the right words, working in the right job, or having the right intentions.

These aren't at all the criteria for peace described in God's Word. Peace is an inner quality that flows out of a right relationship with God.

SPIRITUAL GROWTH

*Grow in the grace and knowledge
of our Lord and Savior Jesus Christ.*
2 PETER 3:18

Spiritual growth is a process. There is an order. Lessons must be learned before other lessons can be assimilated. . . .

I don't know where you are in the process, but God does. He is engineering your circumstances with a definite result in mind. Part of His plan is to bring you to the end of yourself, to a point of desperation where you get so sick of yourself and your inability to change that you throw up your hands in surrender. When that happens, you are closer than you have ever been to knowing the joy of the Spirit-filled life.

BELONGING TO GOD'S CHURCH

Honor all people. Love the brotherhood. Fear God.
1 PETER 2:17

The church is to be a place where people of many spiritual gifts and practical talents can find opportunities to be of service to Christ and can work together to bring about the furtherance of God's kingdom on this earth. The church is to be a place of loving acceptance—not acceptance of sin, but certainly acceptance of sinners. It is to be a place where a person can be appreciated for being a child of God and a special creation of God. Belonging to a church should run far deeper than simply signing a membership roll or attending regularly. Belonging should be a feeling of caring and of serving and of acceptance.

GUIDED BY GOD

The eyes of the LORD are on the righteous,
and His ears are open to their prayers.
1 PETER 3:12

God's plan for your life is that you might be in close fellowship with Him. The means of having that close fellowship is accepting Jesus Christ as your Savior. In accepting Jesus Christ, you are receiving God's forgiveness and opening yourself up to His love.

That's your number one reason for living on this earth—to love God in return. That is the foremost aspect of the destiny God has for you!

Once you have received God's forgiveness . . . then you are ready to fulfill the rest of God's plan for your life, which is this: to follow the Lord wherever He leads you. Your destiny will unfold before you as you obey the daily prompting and leading and guiding of the Holy Spirit.

FOUNDATION OF PEACE

Let the peace of God rule in your hearts.
COLOSSIANS 3:15

None of us are good enough to make it to heaven by our own efforts. Why would Jesus have had to endure death and suffering if we could do it alone? So, God's plan is for all of us, in every generation and in every nation, to ask for His mercy, confess our sins, and trust Him for our salvation. That's the essence of God's plan for you and me, friend. It is also the fundamental requirement for us to experience God's wonderful, continuous gift of peace.

Jesus is the foundation stone of our peace.

GODLY WISDOM

In the way of righteousness is life.
PROVERBS 12:28

All godly wisdom begins with reverence—an understanding of who our sovereign, almighty God is, and out of that understanding, surrendering one's will and behavior to Him. There is no alternative foundation on which genuine wisdom can be built.

A person may say, "Do you mean to tell me that with all of my education and experience, I cannot be wise if I don't receive God's forgiveness for my sin and factor God into my life?" That's exactly what I mean to tell you! And I say this not out of my own human understanding—that's what the Word of God says. Apart from God, a human being *cannot* function in wisdom.

GOD'S FOREVER-LOVE

We have known and believed the love that God has for us.
1 JOHN 4:16

In the end, it is love—and especially the
infinite, unconditional, forgiving love of God
our heavenly Father—that creates in us a feeling
of value and worth. If Jesus, God's Son, went to
the cross for us, surely we are worthy. If Christ
died so that we might live with God forever in a
heavenly home, surely we have value. If God
created us, redeemed us, and desires to call us
His children forever, surely we are of great
importance to Him.

The answer to feelings of unworthiness is
love. An always-and-forever kind of love. A love
that is based not upon what a person does,
but upon who a person is—a beloved child of
almighty God.

THE BODY OF BELIEVERS

Let us not [forsake] the assemblying of ourselves together.
HEBREWS 10:23–25

Everybody on earth wants to be loved and to love someone. When you feel as if you are connected to someone who appreciates you, values you, and loves you, you have feelings of deep tranquillity and calm. . . .

Every person in the body of Christ has been given a unique personality, set of abilities and skills, at least one ministry gift, and natural talents. God expects each of us to share these unique attributes with other believers in a loving, generous way so needs within any particular body of believers will be met and the gospel will be extended to those outside the church. We need one another in the church. We are part of one another.

GOD'S BENEFIT PLAN

*It is God who works in you both
to will and to do for His good pleasure.*
PHILIPPIANS 2:13

God's benefit plan is absolutely fantastic!
Those who accept Christ Jesus as their
personal Savior receive two tremendous benefits:
forgiveness of sin and eternal life. You can't beat
those benefits!

The daily benefits of following Christ are
also tremendous—guidance, provision,
protection, comfort, help in resolving life's
problems, and an outpouring of God's presence.

GOD'S WAY

I will see Your face in righteousness;
I shall be satisfied when I awake in Your likeness.
PSALM 17:15

We must understand that God's primary purpose in our lives is not to meet our needs but to conform us into the likeness of His Son. Many people make God out to be a type of genie, always ready and willing to give them precisely what they desire at any particular moment. They see God as the wish fulfiller, the One who turns all of our dreams into reality, the ultimate fairy godfather, the One who makes all things just the way we desire for them to be. While it is true that God is our Father and our Provider, and while it is equally true that God desires only the best for us for all eternity, God is not present in our lives to do things our way. He is present in our lives so that we might desire and choose to do things His way.

COMMANDMENT OF LOVE

You shall love the LORD your God with all
your heart, with all your soul, and with all your mind.
MATTHEW 22:37

Loving God is a commandment in God's Word because, like following all the commandments, loving God brings good into our lives. It is not a commandment because God fears that we will not love Him unless He commands us to do so. Rather, it is a commandment because God alone is worthy to be loved. It is the only appropriate response to make toward One who loves as He loves. There is no other acceptable or honorable response we can make. It's as if we are being told, "There's only one right thing to do, so do it."

DOING GOD'S WILL

*I do not seek My own will but
the will of the Father who sent Me.*
JOHN 5:30

"What is God's will?" you may ask.
God's will is for you to

- keep His commandments.
- obey His directives about where to go, what to do, what to say.
- take care of the people and things that God has given to you.
- use the natural talents and abilities that God has built into your life.
- use the ministry gifts God imparted to you at the time of your salvation.

BRING ALL THE TITHES

"Bring all the tithes into the storehouse, . . .
and try Me now in this,"   says the LORD of hosts, "If I will
not . . . pour out for you such blessing that there
will not be room enough to receive it."

MALACHI 3:10

God's promise of abundant, overflowing blessing is directly linked to obedience in giving tithes and offerings to Him. . . .

To ask God to bless you financially even though you are in disobedience to His commandments is to ask God to overlook His own laws and statutes and to deny the truthfulness of His Word. God will not do that. Our role is to obey God in all matters, including our giving of tithes and offerings. This is not an area of negotiation. . . . We must never expect God to turn His back on His word for the sake of meeting our personal needs.

A TRANSFORMED LIFE

We pray always for you that . . . the name
of our Lord Jesus Christ may be glorified in you.
2 THESSALONIANS 1:11–12

When we have a friendship with Jesus, our lives take on a completely new quality and nature. We are indwelled by His Holy Spirit. Our lives automatically move away from sin and toward purity. Our lives begin to reflect the character of the Holy Spirit: love, joy, peace, patience, kindness, goodness, faithfulness, gentleness, and self-control (Gal. 5:22–23).

A friend may influence your life, but no human friend can ever totally transform your life from the inside out in the way Jesus Christ does.

A CANDLE IN THE DARK

Let your light so shine before men, that they
may see your good works and glorify your Father in heaven.
MATTHEW 5:16

The life characterized by the fruit of the
Spirit cannot help being noticed. It stands
out like a candle in a dark room. . . .

Today, our world desperately needs to see
men and women whose lives transcend the
norm. The world needs to see husbands and
wives who really love each other. The world
needs to see Christian businessmen and
businesswomen who put honesty before profit
and integrity ahead of a paycheck. . . . Our
world needs to see some fruit. Real fruit.

GOD FILLS THE EMPTINESS

The LORD is your keeper;
the LORD is your shade at your right hand.
PSALM 121:5

No method and no relationship we can ever devise is going to work when it comes to our emotional and spiritual healing. Why? Because God did not make us to go through life on our own. He made us for Himself. He created us to be in fellowship with Him, first and foremost. Certainly God wants us to have good relationships with other people, but the number one relationship for each of us is a relationship with Him.

When we try to get our needs met apart from God, our efforts lead only to disappointment, discouragement, disillusionment, and despair. Only God can fill the emptiness of the human heart. Only God is sufficient to meet our deepest needs for acceptance, love, and worthiness.

OPEN YOUR HEART

*If anyone is in Christ, he is a new creation; old things have
passed away; behold all things have become new.*
2 CORINTHIANS 5:17

The Cross assures you of God's acceptance.
When you believe in Jesus, God considers
all barriers between you and Him to be removed.
Full reconciliation and intimacy of relationship
are possible.

God's acceptance and forgiveness of you, and
God's acceptance and blessing of you, are related
to your acceptance of God. Accepting God's
forgiveness is not a matter of works. It's a matter
of opening your heart, mind, and hands to
receive. There is no earning or striving involved.

WALKING IN CHRIST

As you therefore have received Christ Jesus the Lord,
so walk in Him, rooted and built up
in Him, . . . abounding in it with thanksgiving.
COLOSSIANS 2:6–7

Paul did not say to walk "after" Christ or "in the footsteps of Christ", he said to walk "in" Christ, rooted or abiding in Him. And, Paul added, be grateful for the life you have in Him. Be thankful for this abundant life you have been given in Christ.

When you receive Jesus Christ, the Holy Spirit comes to indwell your spirit, and the very life that you begin to live is His life, manifested through your talents, your gifts, your personality, and in your circumstances and the context of your life.

OBEDIENCE MAKES SENSE

We ought to obey God rather than men.
ACTS 5:29

God's ways don't always appear to make sense! It didn't make sense for Gideon to reduce his armies from thousands to three hundred. It didn't make sense for Joshua to send the Israelites marching silently around the walled city of Jericho as a battle strategy. It didn't make sense for David to go after the champion warrior of the Philistines armed only with a slingshot and a handful of stones.

What God calls us to do may not make sense. We may be able to come up with all sorts of excuses for not obeying. In the end, however, there's only one wise choice: Obey God.

DON'T WORRY!

Do not worry about your life.
MATTHEW 6:25

This is not a suggestion. It is a command. You may say, "But I can't help feeling anxious, I have always been a worrier!" . . . My response is, "Oh, yes you can."

There's nothing about a circumstance that automatically creates anxiety. Anxiety occurs because of the way we respond to a problem or troubling situation. Your ability to choose is part of God's gift of free will to every human being. You can choose how you feel. You can choose what you think about, and you can choose how you will respond to a circumstance.

REDEFINING WHAT IS GOOD

*As the heavens are higher than
the earth, so are My ways higher than your ways.*
ISAIAH 55:9

Our definition of what is good changes as we come to Christ and grow into His likeness. However, God always sees what is absolutely good for us—things that are good for us now, good for us in every area of our lives, good for those around us, and good for us through all eternity. He gives us only the things that are truly beneficial for our growth as His children and that are beneficial for the advancement of His kingdom on this earth.

The question to ask yourself if you have an unmet need today is this: Is this thing that I need something that God defines as good for my life?

DEALING WITH STRESS

The word of the LORD is proven;
He is a shield to all who trust in Him.
PSALM 18:30

Dealing with stress is a matter of perspective and faith. It takes an eternal perspective and God-centered faith. That's a winning combination. Read the stories of the men and women of old. They often faced life-threatening situations. Yet they faced them with perspective and faith of such magnitude that stress found no home in their hearts.

The Spirit-filled life is not a life without responsibility or pressure. It is, however, a life in which God is seen as such a faithful provider that we are free to do what we know to do while trusting Him with those things that are beyond our control.

GOD'S ABIDING PRESENCE

I will never leave you nor forsake you.
HEBREWS 13:5

Jesus never leaves us or forsakes us. He is with us always. . . .

When you are in the valley in despair . . . He's there.

When you arrive at the top of the mountain in triumph . . . He's there.

The old adage is true: When things get thick, friends tend to thin out. That is never true of Jesus, however. He stands by us always. No persecution is ever too intense or criticism too severe for Him to turn away from you. . . . No other friend can ever make that claim.

DELIGHTING IN THE LORD

Delight yourself also in the LORD,
and He shall give you the desires of your heart.
PSALM 37:4

When you delight yourself in another person, you spend as much time as possible with that person, and you get to know that person as well as possible. When you are delighted in your relationship with another person, you are fulfilled, complete, satisfied, content, and joyful in your relationship. If you experience such a relationship, many material and physical things usually become very unimportant. . . .

And so it is when we come to delight in our relationship with the Lord. Nothing else really matters when we experience an intimate time with the Lord. Everything else pales in comparison to Him.

THE ANSWER TO OUR NEEDS

Let all those rejoice who put their trust in You;
let them ever shout for joy, because You defend them.
PSALM 5:11

God told us from the very beginning that in love—His love—we find the answer to all our needs as well as healing for our broken lives.

When your heart is anchored to the heart of Jesus Christ, you will find Him near and always eager to confirm His personal love for you. The love of the world will pass away, but God's love is guaranteed never to fade. He is the Source of all true, lasting love.

ASK IN FAITH

If we know that He hears us, whatever we ask,
we know that we have the petitions that we have asked of Him.
1 JOHN 5:15

Whatever we ask of God . . .

Whatever we voice in thanksgiving to God . . .

Whatever we declare to be the attributes of God . . .

We must offer with faith.

We must truly believe that when we ask of God, He answers.

We must truly believe that He is worthy of all our thanksgiving and praise.

We must truly believe that He is totally capable of handling all things according to the fullness of His plan and purpose for our life.

THE IMPACT OF A GOOD FRIEND

A friend loves at all times.
PROVERBS 17:17

A good friend builds us up so that we want to become and to accomplish all that our friend believes we can be and do. . . .

A good friend can help you become more productive, have a higher energy level, and have more enthusiasm for life. A good friend gives you the confidence to take godly risks, embrace new challenges, and move to the next level in your work or hobby. When you know that someone loves you and is standing with you and believes in you . . . you are far more willing to step out in faith and develop your full potential physically, mentally, emotionally, and spiritually. A good friendship gives you an abiding confidence.

GOD WILL ANSWER

Ask, and you will receive, that your joy may be full.
JOHN 16:24

When I ask God specifically to let me know if something is right or wrong for me, He gives me an answer. If I have no answer, then I assume that I need to do a little more investigating. I need to wait awhile, ask more questions, delve a little deeper, do more research, or probe the situation a little more. Eventually I will come to a point where I *will* hear God's clear answer in my spirit: "Yes, this is something good for you," or "No, this is something to avoid."

A person who is truly seeking the Lord through daily, extensive reading of God's Word and through daily prayer and communication with the Lord—desiring to hear God's answer and to know God's definition of goodness— is going to desire and to ask God for the things that are good in His eyes.

COMPASSION AND COMFORT

He is despised and rejected by men,
a Man of sorrows and acquainted with grief.

ISAIAH 53:3

Our greatest source of comfort is God who, through His Son, Jesus, has identified with us in our sorrow and pain. Our Savior was "a man of sorrows and acquainted with grief." He well understands our situation, our uncertainty, and our fears and through us is able to comfort others.

It is His nature to comfort His children. . . .

He is committed to compassionate care for His children.

APRIL

*God meets our needs
according to His resources.*

A WORTHY GOAL

Commit your way to the LORD,
trust also in Him, and He shall bring it to pass.
PSALM 37:5

Anytime people set goals for their lives that require great striving, intense frustration, repeated failures, and manipulation of others— that is an unrealistic goal. It is not within the realm of their God-given talents and abilities. It is beyond God's plan and purpose for their life.

Now, I'm not saying that the achievement of goals doesn't require effort, education, training, or the development of skills. Those factors are always necessary in the attainment of any goal that is worthy. God doesn't give us talents and abilities that are fully developed. He requires that we sharpen them and mature in their use. It's another thing entirely to commit yourself to becoming an opera singer when you can't carry a tune in a bucket.

FINDING WISDOM

Wisdom is found on the lips of him who has understanding.
PROVERBS 10:13

God's promise is that those who love and search for wisdom *will* find it.

We must take responsibility for applying wisdom to our lives. Those who walk in wisdom feel a responsibility for their actions and use of time. They know they have been given a limited quantity of minutes, hours, days, months, and years. They know they must must spend those hours in a way that produces the largest amount of good. They also know that God has entrusted them with certain material resources that must be used to maximally further God's purposes on the earth.

IT'S NOT WHAT YOU WEAR

We are His workmanship,
created in Christ Jesus for good works.
EPHESIANS 2:10

We have a multibillion-dollar clothing industry in the USA, and it is built upon the premise that looking good is important. We seek to dress well because we are concerned about how others think we look. It is true. We get anxious about our appearance and our performance in life. In other words, many of us worry about how we stack up. . . .

Jesus tells us that our heavenly Father's opinion about who we are is all that truly matters. If He approves of us, that's all the approval we need. He gives us our identity and an inner beauty that far surpasses anything related to what we might wear, own, drive, or live in.

NOWHERE ELSE TO TURN

*Call to Me, and I will answer you, and show
you great and mighty things, which you do not know.*
JEREMIAH 33:3

The Spirit-filled (or Spirit-controlled) life
begins with an overwhelming realization
that we are absolutely helpless and hopeless
apart from the empowerment of the Holy
Spirit. Until that one simple truth grips us at
the core of our being, we will never experience
the power of the Holy Spirit. Why? Because we
will always be out there doing things *for* God in
our strength. . . .

God is an expert at engineering
circumstances so that we find ourselves totally
dependent on Him.

ACCEPTED IN THE BELOVED

He made us accepted in the Beloved.
EPHESIANS 1:6

You cannot earn the status of *accepted* or *included* in the body of Christ. Regardless of what human beings may say or do, God requires nothing but your belief for you to be fully accepted. We human beings often have long lists of works that must be performed, accomplishments that must be earned, or rituals that must be completed before we accept one another into our clubs and organizations. Even on an informal basis, we often set up certain criteria for those we will accept into our clique group or social set. Not so with God! You are fully accepted in the Beloved the moment you receive Jesus Christ as your Savior.

THE FRUIT OF THE SPIRIT

The fruit of the Spirit is love, joy, peace, longsuffering,
kindness, goodness, faithfulness, gentleness, self-control.
GALATIANS 5:22–23

The fruit of the Holy Spirit is first and foremost love. All of the other qualities associated with having the Holy Spirit flow from the presence of God's love in you.

Joy is love enjoying all of the goodness of God. . . . *Peace* is love resting on the promises of God. . . . *Longsuffering* is love waiting for God to reveal to you and in you what He desires to reveal.

Kindness is love reacting to those around you. *Goodness* is love choosing to do what is right . . . in God's eyes.

PROMISE OF PEACE

The peace of God, which surpasses all
understanding, will guard your hearts and minds.
PHILIPPIANS 4:7

To the objective observer, peace is the last emotion in the world Paul *should* have been feeling, but the apostle knew from experience what he was talking about. He had suffered shipwreck and been stoned and lashed on several occasions—all because he was a follower of Jesus. The one foundational truth he knew was that God's peace, though mysterious and impossible to comprehend rationally, is able to see anyone through the journey of life—on a routine day or in the midst of any trial. . . . Peace is a promise of God.

LIFE FROM GOD'S VIEWPOINT

*The eyes of the LORD are in
every place, keeping watch on the evil and the good.*
PROVERBS 15:3

Wisdom is the capacity to see things from God's viewpoint. . . .

God knows what we feel, what we think, who we are, and how we function. He knows our likes, dislikes, dreams, desires, fears, and hurts. He knows what brings us joy, peace, and feelings of fulfillment. As our "Maker" He knows every detail of our "makeup"!

God also knows about every circumstance we encounter. He sees the beginning from the ending, and every step between.

FAILURE AND SUCCESS

He who has the Son has life.
1 JOHN 5:12

The difference between those who have succeeded in spite of their failures and those who have allowed their failures to create low self-worth is this: those who have succeeded have not internalized their failures. They have not thought less of themselves personally for having failed. They have refused to think of themselves as failures or worthless. Failure is something they have done but not something they are. This is a huge difference. In some cases, failures have spurred them on to try harder or to explore new avenues. Those who allow failure to be internalized often give up in their failures and refuse to take the risk of failing again.

One of the most important lessons you will ever learn is this: failure is something you *do*, not something you *are*.

CONFORMED TO CHRIST

Jesus Christ . . . gave Himself for us,
that He might redeem us from every lawless deed.
TITUS 2:13–14

When we approach the promises of God, we must always keep in mind that His ultimate purpose in our lives is to conform us into the image of Jesus Christ. God desires for us the same relationship He had with Jesus— a close intimacy so that we do only what the Father directs and all that we do is for His glory. Jesus was 100 percent obedient to the will of God the Father in all things. He relied exclusively upon God the Father for direction, wisdom, sustenance, provision, and power. Jesus drew His identity solely from God—everything about the character of Jesus the Son was identical to the character of God the Father.

Like Jesus. That is what the Father has in mind for you and for me.

PLEASING GOD

*If any of you lacks wisdom,
let him ask of God, who gives to all liberally.*
JAMES 1:5

Earthly wisdom is limited by man's ability to perceive, to sense, to learn, to understand, to create, and to control. Earthly wisdom is "doing what comes naturally." . . .

Godly wisdom is marked by God's ability to work through mankind. When we allow God to work in us and through us, our abilities to perceive, to sense, to learn, to understand, to create, and to manage life's resources are powerfully expanded.

Godly wisdom is doing what the Holy Spirit compels us to do. It results in what is pleasing to God and ultimately, what is beneficial to man.

LORD OF LORDS

The eye of the LORD is on those who
fear Him, on those who hope in His mercy.
PSALM 33:18

Is Jesus the Lord of everything or only some things? Is He Lord over time, situations, the material universe, and all circumstances? Indeed, He is! Is He Lord over your life? That is a question only you can answer. The truth, however, is that *if* you have made Jesus the Lord of your life, and He is the rightful King of all kings and Lord of all lords, then there isn't a situation, circumstance, or period of time over which Jesus does not have absolute control and sovereignty. He will make certain that all things come together for your good, in His timing and according to His chosen methods, if you will only trust Him completely to be the Lord of your life.

OUR SOURCE AND STRENGTH

In Your hand it is to make great and to give strength to all.
1 CHRONICLES 29:12

The Lord desires to heal you of old emotional wounds and memories, and to heal you so completely that you no longer rely on any of the crutches you have used in the past as a substitute for trust in God. . . .

God alone wants to be the permanent—yes, eternal—solution for every difficulty or problem you encounter. The Lord makes it very clear in His Word that He desires for you to trust in Him alone for your total healing. He is the ultimate and final Source of your strength, healing, and comfort. God wants you to be utterly and completely dependent upon Him, not upon any other person or thing.

LIVING WITHOUT REGRET

*I myself always strive to have
a conscience without offense toward God and men.*
ACTS 24:16

What is the best way to live without regret?

- Choose to live in such a way that you do your best in every task and in every relationship.
- Choose to trust God in every area of your life—every decision, every choice, every opportunity He sends your way.
- Choose to obey God. Keep His commandments.
- Choose to forgive others fully and freely.
- Choose to pursue what God reveals to you as His path for you to follow.

A CLASSIC CASE OF DOUBT

*He who doubts is like a wave of the sea driven
and tossed by the wind. For let not that man suppose that
he will receive anything from the Lord.*

JAMES 1:6–7

The person who asks anything of God without faith is not going to receive what he requests.

I know countless people who make their petitions to God by saying, "God, I know You are all-powerful and all-wise and You can meet all my needs, but . . ." That *but* clause is usually a statement of doubt, not faith. It is a "but in this case" instance of doubt. Many people believe God *can,* but they have doubts that God *will.* They recite to God all of their inadequacies, unworthiness, shame, and inability. God says if you come to Him with that attitude, don't waste your time praying.

GIFTS OF GRACE

*As each one has received a gift, minister it to one
another, as good stewards of the manifold grace of God.*
1 PETER 4:10

Spiritual gifts are God's way of sharing His
grace with others. . . .

For example, when a man loses his wife,
it's comforting for him to know that he will see
her again someday. But that is not nearly as
comforting as having friends around to hold him
and listen and pray. When believers with the gift
of mercy gather around him to listen, when
another with the gift of administration takes care
of all the funeral arrangements, when a neighbor
with the gift of hospitality invites him to spend
several nights with his family, when these things
happen, it is as if Christ Himself reaches down
to take care of one of His own.

CHARLES STANLEY · 117

GOD WILL PROVIDE

Do not worry about tomorrow, for tomorrow will worry about its own things. Sufficient for the day is its own trouble.
MATTHEW 6:34

When we come face-to-face with our inadequacies, failures, and limitations, we are prone to frustration, worry, and anxiety. We don't like recognizing that we cannot control all that we desire to control or that the world does not spin around us.

Jesus said, in effect, "Rather than focus on what *you* desire, which will always lead to the realization of what you cannot do and be in your own strength, turn your attention to what *God* desires! Focus instead on what He can enable you to do and be. Concentrate on what He has prepared for you and desires for you. He will provide!"

BASED ON BELIEF

Blessed are all those who put their trust in Him.
PSALM 2:12

Your relationship with God is not based upon your good deeds. It is not based upon your offering of a blood sacrifice at a designated shrine, your doing a series of charitable acts of kindness, or your belonging to a particular denomination. It is not based upon anything that you produce, achieve, or earn.

Rather, your relationship with God is based upon belief—believing that Jesus Christ is God's Son come in the flesh and that Jesus Christ is Lord.

Behavior is the substance of religion. Belief is the substance of relationship.

JESUS PRAYS FOR US

The LORD knows the thoughts of man.
PSALM 94:11

One of the attributes of Jesus is that He knows the hearts of men and understands what goes on in our spirits. (See Mark 2:6 and Luke 9:47.) In knowing our hearts, Jesus perceives our motivations, desires, and yearnings as well as our inadequacies, ineptitudes, and deficiencies. He sees what we need. Out of His deep love for us, Jesus brings our needs to the Father.

The Father always responds to what Jesus brings to Him. There is no prayer that Jesus prays on our behalf that goes unheeded or unanswered by the Father. So even though we have not brought our need to Jesus, Jesus brings our need to the Father, and the Father takes action on our behalf, for our good, in order to meet our need.

A TREMENDOUS TREASURE

Search for [wisdom] as for hidden treasures;
then you will understand the fear of the LORD.
PROVERBS 2:4–5

I can guarantee you that if I announced from the pulpit one Sunday that I knew with certainty that any person who would travel one hour north of Atlanta on a certain highway, turn onto a specific dirt road, travel four and one-half miles, turn onto another dirt road and travel one hundred yards, park under a giant tree to the right of the road, and then dig down four feet would find a million dollars' worth of old silver coins . . . the church auditorium would empty quickly! People would be eager to get their tools together, fill up the car with gasoline, and head out to search for such a tremendous treasure.

God says that wisdom is more valuable than any amount of tangible treasure. Are you willing to make the effort to search for His wisdom?

CALLED BY GOD

All things work together for good to those who love God,
to those who are the called according to His purpose.
ROMANS 8:28

That verse clearly tells us that God has a purpose for each one of us. He calls us to it. But to be one who qualifies as "those who are called" implies that we are walking in that calling, obeying God, and yielding to the direction of the Holy Spirit on a daily basis. If we are truly being obedient to God's commands and we are following His purpose for our lives to the best of our abilities, then God is fully committed to working all things together for our good—both our eternal rewards and our earthly blessings.

GOD'S STOREHOUSE

*I am God, your God! . . . Every beast
of the forest is Mine, and the cattle on a thousand hills.*
PSALM 50:7

God meets our needs according to His resources. And what are God's resources?

My! You cannot begin to count all of God's resources. The oceans and seas are His. The continents are His. The atmosphere and all of outer space are His. All that is under the continents and all that is locked away as potential for life-giving blessing in plants and animals— *His!* We cannot begin to calculate all of God's resources that are available for His use on this earth, and we haven't even begun to count the unseen resources of heaven. His resources are immeasurable, indestructible, and inexhaustible.

DISCERNMENT FOR DECISIONS

*Happy is he who has the God of Jacob
for his help, whose hope is in the LORD his God.*
PSALM 146:5

The Holy Spirit helps believers discern between what is true and what is not; what is wise and what is foolish; what is best and what is simply acceptable. Each day is full of decisions. Most of our decisions concern issues not clearly spelled out in the Scriptures. For example, where to attend school, whether to hire a particular applicant, how much to budget for vacation, and on it goes.

As you are barraged with the details of everyday living, the Holy Spirit will guide you. He will give you that extra-on-the-spot sense of discernment you need to make both big and small decisions.

CHOOSE GOD'S WAY

It is God who works in you both
to will and to do for His good pleasure.
PHILIPPIANS 2:13

How can you determine if you should continue walking on the path God has set you on?

Get God's viewpoint.

Do what the Word of God tells you to do.

Follow the promptings of the Holy Spirit.

Determine in your heart that you will choose God's way over your own way.

Persevere in what God directs you to do. And you will walk in wisdom . . . all the way to eternity's door.

DOING OUR PART

I delight to do Your will,
O my God, and Your law is within my heart.
PSALM 40:8

What is the way out of a circumstance created by an unwise decision? A wise decision. And who is primarily responsible for meeting the need? The person who has made the unwise decision.

What is God's role in this? . . . I believe that God will give daily guidance to any person who requests it, and that He will give courage, fortitude, and willpower to any person who requests these qualities. . . .

He will not do our part, but He will assist us so that our efforts will succeed and we will have both the courage and the endurance necessary to see a problem resolved fully or a need fully met.

TRUE PEACE

Cast your burden on the LORD, and He shall sustain you;
He shall never permit the righteous to be moved.
PSALM 55:22

From the world's perspective, there are many places you can go to find comfort. But there is only one place you will find a hand to catch your tears and a heart to listen to your every longing. True peace comes only from God. No situation is so great that God is not greater still.

Is urgency in your heart? Something that threatens your emotional well-being as well as your ability to perform in life? Take it to Jesus.

SAFE IN GOD'S ARMS

He who promised is faithful.
HEBREWS 10:23

Focus on God's unconditional love for you and anybody else who may be involved in the crisis you face. Focus on His power and ability to control all circumstances. Focus on His always-listening ear that hears you and His always-watchful eye that sees you day and night.

Remember this: The larger your thoughts about God, the smaller your thoughts about your problem!

Refuse to have a pity party or slide into depression. Choose instead to see God's loving arms wrapped around you, lifting you up to safety, provision, and peace!

HELPMATE AND FRIEND

It is not good that man should be alone;
I will make him a helper comparable to him.

GENESIS 2:18

History bears out the truth that most highly successful men have a woman in their lives who loves them, motivates them, encourages them, and helps them to achieve their best and highest. It may be a mother, a sister, an aunt, or a wife. Every good marriage I have ever witnessed bears this quality that both the husband and the wife encourage each other to walk in godly wisdom and to be and do their very best.

The creation of Eve was about far more than God providing a sexual companion for Adam. Eve shared the totality of Adam's life. She was a helper "comparable to him" and he, in turn, was of help to her (Gen. 2:20). They shared not only a garden home, but also a purpose for living and a responsibility before God.

HEARTS TURNED TO GOD

He gives wisdom to the wise and
knowledge to those who have understanding.
DANIEL 2:21

Whatever wisdom you have, you got from God. Only God can truly reveal how to apply knowledge and understanding to the practical issues of life. Furthermore, whatever knowledge you are able to take in and assimilate into your life is made possible because of the ability God has given you to discern, perceive, and understand.

We do not think in a vacuum. Ideas may seem to come out of nowhere, but in truth, they have a source—either God or the enemy of our souls working in the imagination and lustful desires. Feelings may seem to erupt spontaneously, but in truth, they have a source—the heart, which is turned toward or away from God.

COMFORTERS WHO CARE

Blessed be . . . the Father of mercies and God
of all comfort, who comforts us in all our tribulation.
2 CORINTHIANS 1:3–4

The best comforters are those who have been through trouble and tragedy themselves. They know the feelings, the sadness, and the emotional upheavals that go with the territory. So when we go through adversity, isn't it reassuring to have someone there to walk with us who has endured the same trauma we are experiencing? Especially comforting is the friend who reminds us that our God is "the Father of all comfort" who has promised never to leave us or to forsake us.

MAY

*God leads to
what is absolutely right.*

LED BY THE SPIRIT

*May the Lord direct your hearts into
the love of God and into the patience of Christ.*

2 THESSALONIANS 3:5

God can and will speak to your conscience if you allow Him to do so. The Holy Spirit within you will always nudge you toward God's commandments and His goodness. He will always move you toward God's love and toward what is right in God's eyes. God's Word declares that the work of the Holy Spirit is to "direct your hearts into the love of God and into the patience of Christ." He will not lead you to do what is wrong; rather He will lead you to what is absolutely, clearly, and definitively right— not only for you in the moment, but for you and all other believers in Christ Jesus for all eternity.

GOD MEETS OUR NEEDS

He has sent Me to heal the brokenhearted.
ISAIAH 61:1

One of the reasons that God came in the form of human flesh, in the life of His Son, Jesus Christ, was to show us that He is concerned about human need. Jesus Christ identified with human need. He confronted, dealt with, and fought against human need of all types. Jesus did not sit afar off, passing judgment on those in need or ignoring the needs of the people. To the contrary! He rolled up His sleeves and marched straight forward into the greatest needs known to man.

MAY 3

YOUR MENTAL GRID

Your word is a lamp to my feet and a light to my path.
PSALM 119:105

Each of us has a mental grid—all that we have been taught has been placed on that grid, and this grid functions as a filter for evaluating new information. . . .

Some of us have faulty grids. We have been taught incorrectly in the past. Anytime you find something in the Word of God that doesn't match your mental grid, it is time to change your grid. The Bible is our sourcebook for truth. It holds out to us the mental grid we all should have been taught.

The more we hear information, the more frequently we encounter concepts, the more deeply that input is etched into our minds. That's why it is so important to read the Bible daily and repeatedly.

WHAT WE CHOOSE TO THINK

*Whatever things are true, whatever things are noble, . . .
whatever things are of good report, . . .—meditate on these
things . . . and the God of peace will be with you.*
PHILIPPIANS 4:8–9

Meditating on the good things of life
means that your mind is dominated by,
permeated by, totally captivated by, and fully
occupied by good ideas, concepts, and insights.

What does this mean to us in a practical
sense? When we choose to think about those
things that inspire us, encourage us, teach us,
and build us up emotionally, we find that we
want to follow God's will and we will desire to
remain faithful to Him.

When we choose to think about the majesty
and glory of God, we rely upon Him with
increasing faith and trust.

THE CHANGE AGENT

It is God who works in you,
both to will and to do for His good pleasure.

PHILIPPIANS 2:13

The Holy Spirit is a change agent. Change is what He is all about. He took a man who made his living destroying churches and changed him into the greatest church planter of all time! He took a group of uneducated fishermen and changed them into world-class evangelists and pastors. Through the years He has indwelt men and women with every imaginable habit, reputation, and persuasion and changed them into people of excellence. And he will do the same for you.

GOD'S TENDER EMBRACE

*As the bridegroom rejoices over
the bride, so shall your God rejoice over you.*
ISAIAH 62:5

Oh, how our heavenly Father longs to have you run to His arms, to accept His acceptance, and to enjoy His presence. You have been given the ability and prerogative to ignore Him, continue on your own way, and rebel against His desire for your close fellowship. But why not look at Him fully and see the love He has for you? . . . Why not choose to be the recipient of His love and to accept His relationship?

Perhaps you are reluctant to believe God accepts you fully because you are afraid that you might one day lose His acceptance and love. Nothing, my friend—absolutely nothing—can destroy your acceptance by God or diminish His love extended to you. Not now, not ever.

A LASTING WORK

He who has begun a good work
in you will complete it until the day of Jesus Christ.
PHILIPPIANS 1:6

Anything that God does in your life will last. It will be for your perfection, your wholeness. And it will endure throughout all the ages. What Christ is doing in you, day by day, week in and week out, year in and year out, is a good work that has eternal value. You are not only a work in progress, but you are a good work in progress. God is building into you the qualities of Himself that will last forever.

The Lord is utterly committed to the work in you, and the work that He is doing is a good work with eternal benefit!

GOD'S IN CONTROL

He shall call upon Me, and I will
answer him; I will be with him in trouble.
PSALM 91:15

We may not completely understand God's purposes, but we can be assured of this— God is still in control. He hasn't lost one measure of His power or might. He is just as omnipotent, omniscient, omnipresent, and all loving today as He was the day before September 11, 2001.

The godly response to tragedies such as those that occurred 9/11 are not the questions "Why did this happen?" or "Why did God allow this?" The godly response is to ask, "God, what do you want me to learn in response to this?"

GOD MOVES IN MYSTERY

*As the heavens are higher than
the earth, so are My ways higher than your ways.*
ISAIAH 55:9

Earthly wisdom is rooted in the belief that all of life can be understood, rationalized, and proved scientifically. But God moves in ways that are still a mystery to man. Science can never prove what causes a person to fall in love. It can never prove what happens to a person after death. It can never measure the breadth or depth of God's love and mercy. . . .

None of the world's information we have acquired or the tangible skills we have developed in order to acquire, maintain, and advance our lives on this earth will be useful in eternity. The wisdom of this world has no capability to carry a person from this life into the next.

CONFESSING SIN

*I acknowledged my sin to You,
and my iniquity I have not hidden.*
PSALM 32:5

The only way to deal definitively with guilt is to confess the sin associated with it. A person must go to God and say, "I acknowledge this sin, and I own up to it before You, God. I ask You to forgive me for my sin and to wash this sin from my conscience and from my soul."

If you have uneasy needy feelings in your life, I encourage you to examine your past and to face any unconfessed sin. Allow God to forgive you and to free you. In receiving God's forgiveness, you are also receiving God's love, which declares you to be worthy of His forgiveness and love. Only in Christ Jesus can genuine worthiness be found.

BE YOUR BEST

*You are our Father; we are the clay, and You
our potter; and all we are the work of Your hand.*
ISAIAH 64:8

God expects us to change whatever it takes to be our best at all that we do. He wants us to look our best, dress our best, speak our best, act our best, try our best, give our best, and work to the best of our ability and energy. It is important to understand that the term *best* is related to your own potential, not a term of comparison with others. Your best has nothing to do with another person's best. Furthermore, your best today is not likely to be your best tomorrow. We all can improve certain aspects of our lives, and continue to improve them every day for the rest of our lives.

MAKING WISE DECISIONS

*He guards the paths of justice,
and preserves the way of His saints.*
PROVERBS 2:8

Most of us make mistakes because we do not know the right choice or decision to make. We do not consciously say, "I am now going to make a mistake." Rather, we tend to make mistakes by being careless regarding the needs or desires of others, by not asking the right questions, or by not taking into consideration all the factors that are important to consider. . . .

When we seek God's wisdom, He leads us to decisions that are right, just, equitable, and good not only for us personally, but for everybody involved.

PLANNING WITH PRAYER

If the Lord wills, we shall live and do this or that.
JAMES 4:15

Have you ever considered that the Lord can cause any storm in your life to blow you to the place where He intends for you to arrive? Many of us think that it is up to us to decide where we are going to be five years from now, or even that it is up to us to decide exactly what we are going to do tomorrow, next week, or next year. If we claim Jesus as our Lord, then those decisions are up to Him, not us. We can make plans, and we are wise to do so, but our plans must always be the result of prayer and made with total flexibility that if this is not what God desires for us to do, we will be quick to alter our course.

COVERED WITH GOD'S LOVE

That you . . . may be able to . . .
know the love of Christ which passes knowledge.
EPHESIANS 3:17–19

God's love for you is inexhaustible and beyond any form of measurement. It cannot be multiplied, added, divided, or subtracted. . . .

God loves us more than our pain hurts us. He covers our wound with His love. No matter how much others might criticize us, reject us, or cause us harm, if we turn to God in our pain, He extends to us enough love to completely compensate for the pain. We turn to Him with a pound of pain, and He gives us back two pounds of love. He gives us enough love not only to heal us but to provide an overflow of love that we can extend to the very people who hurt us!

THE HEART OF PEACE

God is not the author of confusion but of peace.
1 CORINTHIANS 14:33

Trusting God is at the heart of peace.
Think for a moment about a young child or baby lying peacefully . . . in the mother's arms. That baby has a total sense of trust that the mother's arms are secure. Her trust allows her to rest in peace.

If a child, however, is in the arms of a stranger—someone she doesn't know and therefore doesn't trust—that child will be agitated, fussy, nervous, and is likely to begin crying in anxiety. She doesn't have peace.

The same principle applies to us. When we have any opinion about God that diminishes our trust of Him, we are going to feel anxious.

WORTHY OF GOD'S LOVE

That the world may know that You have
sent Me, and have loved them as You have loved Me.
JOHN 17:23

How does someone know that he is valuable? The answer is to be found when one looks at the cross. When a person comes face-to-face with the cross and confronts the fullness of its reality, that person comes face-to-face with his own value.

How much are you worth?

You are worth so much that God sent Jesus to die in your place on the cross.

OVERCOMING FAITH

This is the victory that has overcome the world—our faith.
1 JOHN 5:4

If you will begin every day with a declaration of victory over the specific giants in your life, you will experience victory. Begin tomorrow morning on your knees. Think through the temptations you will face, the pressure you will feel, and the rejection you are likely to encounter. Item by item, thank God for the victory. Remind Him that at the cross Christ paid the price not only for your sin but for your victory.

By doing so, you activate your faith before activating your will to resist on your own. When the temptation or pressure comes, tell the Holy Spirit, "Christ has already dealt with this, and I have already claimed His power, so handle it through me."

ASK AND RECEIVE

*"I did not come to call the righteous,
but sinners, to repentance."*
MATTHEW 9:13

Are you aware that Jesus did not heal every sick person in the land of Palestine when He walked the earth? Jesus healed these sick people who were brought to Him or who came to Him. . . .

People who recognize that they are sick seek help. Those who recognize they need forgiveness confess their sins and repent of their sinful lives.

Even though God confronts every person with his neediness at some point in his life, God never forces anyone to accept the healing and wholeness He offers. He does not move beyond the boundaries of human will.

GOD'S THRONE ROOM

*Come to me, all you who labor
and are heavy laden, and I will give you rest.*
MATTHEW 11:28

Through the Cross, God has made Himself totally available to you—sixty minutes an hour, twenty-four hours a day, every day of every year of your life.

Jesus invites you to come boldly into the throne room of God and to find grace and mercy for help in your times of need. He makes God completely accessible. . . .

God is available to you whenever you turn to Him.

HELP FROM GOD'S SERVANTS

"Be of good cheer! It is I; do not be afraid."
MATTHEW 14:27

An old and familiar story is told of a young child who was troubled by a thunderstorm. She sought refuge in her parents' bedroom as the lightning flashed and the thunder rolled in the night sky. Her parents hugged her and cuddled her and attempted to comfort her by saying, "You are going to be all right. God is with you. He will take care of you." The little girl replied, "Yes, but I still want to be with someone who has arms."

In many cases, I have seen God provide someone "with arms" to comfort those who are grieving, those who are troubled, or those who are sick or suffering. God sends His ministering servants to those in need as an expression of His reassurance and comfort.

THE STANDARD

Great peace have those who love
Your law, and nothing causes them to stumble.
PSALM 119:165

We need to personalize and apply the Bible to our lives, and not only once but repeatedly, day in and day out. . . .

Allow the Word of God to persuade you. Allow the Word of God to influence your thinking. Allow the Word of God to alert your perspective and change your behavior.

No matter what any human being may say to us, if any part of that message does not line up with the Word of God, it needs to be dismissed. The Word of God is the standard by which all instruction should be evaluated.

GETTING ALONG WITH OTHERS

Beloved, if God so loved us, we also ought to love one another.
1 JOHN 4:11

A person once said to me, "I don't think God expects me to get along with people who have a personality I don't like."

Yes, He does.

Getting along with a person should have nothing to do with personality. There's no place in Scripture where personality negates our obligation to show kindness, mercy, forgiveness, civility, or good manners! Personality should make no more difference than age, race, sex, culture, nationality, or any other defining factor.

CREATED IN GOD'S IMAGE

*God created man in His
own image; in the image of God He created him.*
GENESIS 1:27

God created us to be spiritual and emotional beings. In that way we are most like God—in the spiritual, inner dimension we have been created "in His own image." The spiritual, emotional, psychological nature is the foremost aspect of who we are. It is the part of us that has a capacity for eternity. After having created this essential and vital aspect of man's being, God then put man in a physical body, set him into a natural environment, gave him material substance, and blessed him with human companions. When we neglect or negate the emotional and spiritual part of who God made us to be, we are immediately in a state of need, lack, want, and disharmony.

UNLOAD YOUR CARES

Be anxious for nothing, but in everything
by prayer and supplication with thanksgiving let your
requests be made known to God;
and the peace of God . . . shall guard your hearts.
PHILIPPIANS 4:6–7

"Don't worry. Pray!" Paul says. And notice the immediate result—peace. Even before our prayers are answered, there is peace. Before we have any idea how things will work out, there is peace. Why? Because by crying out to God and unloading our cares and burdens on Him, He is assured of (and we are reminded of) our dependence on Him. And that is what pleases Him.

RESISTING TEMPTATION

The devil walks about like a roaring lion,
seeking whom he may devour. Resist him, steadfast in the faith.
1 PETER 5:8–9

The sequence for every temptation we face is thought, fantasy, desire, choice, and willful decision to yield. The process may happen very quickly—in a matter of seconds at times. . . .

The best time to put a stop to any temptation is when it is still an idea. We need to confront temptation to sin with an idea that is godly. That godly idea may be a prayer for God's help . . . a refocusing of the mind on a goal that the Lord has set before us . . . or a verse of Scripture that we repeat to ourselves aloud. . . .

Memorize verses to recite in the face of temptation. Prepare yourself in advance so that when the white-hot moment of temptation comes, you will have a full scriptural arsenal as part of your response.

LOOKING TO GOD

*In His love . . . He bore them
and carried them all the days of old.*
ISAIAH 63:9

When we talk about having our needs met,
we human beings often look to everyone
except to God. We seek answers from relatives,
friends, and a host of other sources—some helpful,
others harmful to our spirits—rather than look
to God.

The ultimate source for meeting all need is
God. He uses a variety of methods and
instruments to meet our needs, but He is the
Author and Originator of all that we need, both
in the outer material, natural, and physical
realm, and in the inner emotional, mental,
and spiritual realm.

LET GOD HANDLE IT

*As the heavens are high above the earth,
so great is His mercy toward those who fear Him.*
PSALM 103:11

Adversity can be handled one of two ways. Either you can deal with it on your own, or you can allow God to carry your burden for you. The first requires human strength and effort, which are rarely sufficient in handling grievous trials. Heartache erodes human ability.

The wiser course of action is to allow God to handle your adversity. His ability to provide goes beyond our greatest imagination. He is the God who has the ability to calm every storm.

ROCK-SOLID FRIENDSHIP

There is a friend who sticks closer than a brother.
PROVERBS 18:24

People need people. We each need relationships with others who are "comparable to us"—like us in values, desires, goals, beliefs, and to a degree, personality—so that we might receive help from them and help them in return. We need other people in order to grow into the fullness of our own potential and in order that we might experience a mutual giving and receiving of love and kindness. . . .

A real friend is one who sticks closer than a brother—he will be there through thick and thin, in good times and bad. He will provide strength so that you do not crumble in the face of evil or calamity. He remains rock-solid and steadfast in times of trauma.

SEEKING GOD

But as for me, I would seek God.
JOB 5:8

When we seek the Lord, He makes Himself known to us. He is forever accessible and available to those who seek Him.

We are wise to seek God anytime we have sinned, and to do so with prayer, fasting, and a genuinely humble heart.

We are wise to seek God anytime we face danger.

We must seek God with a humility of heart and with a desire to have a greater manifestation of righteousness in our hearts.

We are always to seek God as our first priority

LIVING LIKE CHRIST

*He who believes in Me, the works that I do he
will do also; and greater works than these he will do.*
JOHN 14:12

Jesus challenged His disciples to be perfect—
to be made whole and complete—to lay down
their old lives and pick up the new life He
would give them.

No friend will ever challenge you to the
heights that Jesus challenges you. . . .Whatever
Jesus commands us to do, He enables us to do.
He is a Friend who not only tells us what to do,
but a Friend who walks through life with us every
step of the way, guiding us and empowering us to
live out the life He Himself led.

OUR HEAVENLY GIFT-GIVER

*If you then, being evil, know how to give good gifts
to your children, how much more will your Father who is
in heaven give good things to those who ask Him!*
MATTHEW 7:11

A good parent gives gifts that are appropriate to a child's development and maturity. A good parent gives gifts that will be a blessing to a child and will not cause the child harm. And so it is with God. He gives us the gifts that are appropriate for us according to our spiritual ability to handle the gifts in such a way that they are a blessing and not harmful.

Good gifts are the only kind that God can or will give.

JUNE

*God's commandments
are for our good always.*

TALENTS USED FOR GOD

The LORD will perfect that which concerns me.
PSALM 138:8

God desires for us to become all that He created us to be. He expects us to develop and then to use all of the talents, abilities, and gifts that He has placed within us. He intends for us to maximize our potential—to become the man or woman He created us to be.

God's plan is for us to accomplish all of the work that He sets before us. He does not call us to unfinished tasks or halfhearted ventures. When God places a challenge, opportunity, or goal in front of us, He expects us to pursue it with our whole heart, mind, and soul and to experience a measure of success in accomplishing what He has called us to do.

SAVED FROM OURSELVES

"It is no longer I who live, but Christ lives in me."
GALATIANS 2:20

God never intended for His children to live a life characterized by defeat. He doesn't expect you to live with defeat in your thought life, your emotions, your attitudes, your self-control, or your faith. He paid much too high a price to allow you into His family just to watch you fail in your attempts to function as His family member.

God's plan of salvation includes a provision for saving you from yourself. And the key player in that part of His plan is the Holy Spirit. The Holy Spirit is God's provision for righteous living. He is the abiding presence of Christ's life in you. That is why Paul could say with confidence, "It is no longer I who live, but Christ lives in me."

THE MASTER CRAFTSMAN

You formed my inward parts;
You covered me in my mother's womb.
PSALM 139:13

Think for a moment about a carpenter who is getting ready to build a house. He has the blueprints in hand. He has acquired all of the materials necessary, including all of the lumber. He looks at his tools and says, "For this particular job, I need a hammer." And he pulls out a hammer and begins to use it. In a similar fashion, God had a job in mind that needed to be done this year, in your particular area of the world. He created you to be His tool, His instrument, His vessel in getting that job done. He made you from your birth to be fully equipped, fashioned, and prepared for doing the job He had planned.

GOD KNOWS US

The LORD commanded us to observe all these statutes,
to fear the LORD our God, for our good always.
DEUTERONOMY 6:24

God's commandments are always for our good. God made us, and He knows our limitations, our drives, our weaknesses. He also knows what will give us the greatest sense of fulfillment, satisfaction, meaning, purpose, and hope. He knows what will put us into the best possible position to give and receive love from other people. His commandments are His operating instructions so that we might experience all of the wonderful things that He desires to give us.

A SEASON AND A REASON

I have come that they may have life,
and that they may have it more abundantly.

JOHN 10:10

The assurance of Jesus is that because God is with us, we do not have to give in to, sink beneath, or become defeated by troubles. We can face them, confront them, challenge them, deal with them, and in the end overcome them! What consolation this should bring to our hearts.

Jesus taught His followers that all challenges are passing in nature. Sickness and trouble are for a season and for a reason. . . . Jesus' very life was for a season and a reason. Even His death and burial in a tomb were only for a season and a reason!

WE NEED GOD'S WISDOM

Keep sound wisdom and discretion;
so they will be life to your soul.
PROVERBS 3:21-22

We walk two congruent and simultaneous paths in life: We walk *with* God, and we walk *with* other people. We need wisdom primarily about *how* to walk wisely in our relationship with God and to grow in our relationship with Him. We need God's wisdom about *how* to build relationships that are deep, lasting, purposeful, and godly. Although we certainly need God's best strategies for dealing with other practical areas of life, these two areas of wisdom are paramount to every person, every day.

HEAVEN'S UNDERSTANDING

*We also speak, not in words which man's
wisdom teaches but which the Holy Spirit teaches.*

1 CORINTHIANS 2:13

The wisdom given by the Holy Spirit yields clarity and precision. It leads to an expansion of ability, a righteous perspective, and the establishment of goals that are focused and productive, and that are centered on the most important things of eternal benefit.

The presence of the Holy Spirit expands a person's ability to perceive so that a person "sees" life in the context of eternity. The person who walks in godly wisdom does not make decisions on the basis of how things look on the surface at any given time. What he perceives is placed against the template of heaven's understanding and will.

CHRIST, OUR STRENGTH

I can do all things through Christ who strengthens me.
PHILIPPIANS 4:13

Paul wrote to the Philippians, "I can do all things through Christ who strengthens me." Does that mean that Paul could do all things? Was he talented in every area of life? No. Paul was the first to admit his weaknesses and failures. But Paul could do *all things through Christ who strengthened him*. Paul could do whatever the Lord empowered and enabled him to do. He was completely reliant upon God to do His work in him and through him.

You, too, can do whatever Him leads you to do if you trust in Him to give you the ability and the power to do it. Nothing is beyond the realm of possibility if you trust God to help you fulfill His plan for your life. When God gives us a destination point, He will give us the road on which to travel.

UNIQUELY YOU

Do not neglect the gift that is in you.
1 TIMOTHY 4:14

At the time you accepted Jesus Christ as your Savior, God gave you certain spiritual gifts to use in ministry to others. The way in which you express those gifts is uniquely linked to the talents He has given you and the skills He has helped you develop.

Nobody who has lived before you has been just like you. No one alive on the earth today is just like you, not even a sibling who is your twin. Nobody who will ever live will be just like you, including your children. You are a unique and very special creation of God, designed for a particular purpose on this earth that God has had in mind from eternity past. Accept who God made you to be!

WALKING BY GOD'S WORD

Let us hold fast the confession of our hope without wavering.
HEBREWS 10:23

Left to our own devices, we tend to lie to ourselves—we deceive ourselves into hearing what we want to hear, doing what is pleasing to our senses, and pursuing what makes us feel happy.

When we seek to live according to God's wisdom, we are saying to our emotions: "I walk by faith, not by sight. I will not base every decision on the way that I feel—or the way that I think a certain decision will cause me to feel. I will walk by what the Word of God says. I am going to trust the Holy Spirit to guide me, not my own desires, impulses, and emotions."

THE DETAILS

*Jesus made His disciples get into the boat
and go before Him to the other side.*
MATTHEW 14:22

Jesus insisted that the disciples get into the
boat and go before Him to the other side. . . .
He did not tell them their time of arrival.
Neither did He tell them how He was getting
to the other side of the sea. He said, "Get in the
boat, row to the other side, and I'll meet you
over there."

The Lord may not tell you every detail of
His plan. Your position is not to require every
detail or to know all things, but to obey what
God tells you to do. How the Lord does His
part, and what His timing may be, is God's
business, not yours.

GOD'S MOTIVE IS LOVE

God so loved the world that He gave His only begotten Son.
JOHN 3:16

The very essence of God's being—His personality, His nature—is love. The motivation for Him sending Jesus into the world was love. The most famous verse in all the Bible tells us this: "God so loved the world that He gave His only begotten Son" (John 3:16).

The reason Jesus came to this earth, lived a victorious life, and then died as the one definitive and lasting sacrifice to reunite God and human beings was love. God desires to have a relationship with you. He desires to reveal Himself to you, to shower His love and good gifts upon you, and to live with you forever.

DEPEND ON GOD'S WORD

My tongue shall speak of Your word,
for all Your commandments are righteousness.
PSALM 119:172

The person who doesn't trust the accuracy and truthfulness of God's Word is a person who has no foundation for finding, receiving, or accepting God's offer of peace. Without the Bible there is no basis on which to trust God, receive God's forgiveness, or know with certainty what is right and wrong. There's no foundation for a genuine understanding about how to develop an ongoing relationship with God or a peaceful fellowship with others outside His word.

CHRIST IN ME!

*God willed to make known . . . this mystery
among the Gentiles: which is Christ in you, the hope of glory.*
COLOSSIANS 1:27

Christ in me is the ultimate proclamation of self-value!

The person who has a deep and abiding sense of self-worth can hear all kinds of criticism and cutting remarks from other people and let the negative comments just slide off him. He can go on about his life's work with joy because he has an inner confidence that says, "So much for your opinion. I know *God* loves me, and His opinion of my value never diminishes, never changes, and is the only opinion that truly counts." Your critics, your detractors, and your enemies have no hold on you when you draw your identity, your help, and your sense of worth from God Himself.

FORGIVE AND MOVE ON

Blessed are you when they revile and persecute you,
and say all kinds of evil against you falsely for My sake.
MATTHEW 5:11

When Spirit-filled believers are treated unjustly, they feel the outrage and frustration that accompany such acts. There may even be a period of time in which thoughts of revenge cloud their thinking. But before long, they regain perspective. They refocus on the truth. They remind themselves that "all things . . . work together for good" (Rom. 8:28), and that as believers, they are not to repay evil for evil (see 1 Pet. 3:9). Again, they don't deny the pain; they just look at it differently. They choose not to become bitter. They forgive and move on.

GOOD THINGS

He who did not spare His own Son,
but delivered Him up for us all, how shall He not
with Him also freely give us all things.
ROMANS 8:32

The good things that God the Father has for Jesus, He has for us!

Too many Christians seem to believe that life should be a tedious, long-faced journey— no laughter, no fun, no pleasure. . . .

A person who is walking in obedience to God should have abundant reasons to enjoy life. God desires for His children to have a life overflowing with all things that are good, and certainly laughter, joy, beauty, comfort, creative expression, blessing, love, health, friendships, and adventures can be very good things in our lives.

ALWAYS NEAR GOD'S LOVE

Neither death nor life . . .
shall be able to separate us from the love of God.
ROMANS 8:38–39

There is nothing that can separate you from God.

The mistakes you make and the sins you commit after you have accepted Christ Jesus do not separate you from God. He will convict you of these sins so you can confess them, be forgiven, repent of them, and make a change in your future behavior—for your sake, for your good. But these sins do not separate you again from God. God told His people that even if they disobeyed Him and experienced all the negative consequences, He would still be there when they turned to Him. He continually called Himself "the LORD your God." They never ceased being His people.

THE STARTING POINT

As many as touched Him were made well.
MARK 6:56

God does not place needs within our lives so that we will be imperfect, incomplete human beings. These needs exist within us to compel us to seek God and to rely upon Him to make us whole. . . . Our needs, in other words, become our potential. In the resolving and the overcoming of needs through the power of the Holy Spirit, we truly come into the fullness of all that we were created to accomplish, achieve, and fulfill in our lives. Our needs are the launching platform for us to accomplish the purpose for our lives. They are the starting point for us to learn, grow, develop, and eventually come into the fullness of the stature of Christ Jesus.

A PEACE-FILLED HEART

The heavens will praise Your wonders,
O LORD; Your faithfulness also in the assembly of the saints.
PSALM 89:5

You cannot predict tomorrow. You cannot fully prepare for all of its contingencies. You cannot fully provide for all you'll need in your future. God not only can, He already has! God is never caught off guard. He is never taken by surprise. He never comes up short. So you do not have to live with anxiety about the future. The peace-filled heart is the one that recognizes "My times are in His hands."

EMOTIONAL WOUNDS

*You know my sitting down and my
rising up; You understand my thought afar off.*
PSALM 139:2

Only God can heal deep inner emotional wounds, especially ones that stem from early childhood. Some incidents occur at such an early age that the victim of abusive, neglectful, or hurtful behavior cannot even remember what happened or the context in which it happened. Only God sees the beginning from the ending in a person's life. Only God knows *why* some feelings exist in us. Only God knows *how* to unravel the tangled web of emotions that trap us into despair and despondency.

MY WILL OR GOD'S?

"Not as I will, but as You will."
MATTHEW 26:39

From God's perspective, the content of our prayers takes second place to the question of whether or not we are willing to obey Him. His ultimate goal is hearts and minds that are in complete harmony with His kingdom agenda. His plan for you and me is to move us to the place where we can sincerely say with Christ, "Not as I will, but as You will."

OUR HELPER

He will give you another Helper, . . . the Spirit of truth.
JOHN 14:16–17

We need the Holy Spirit, whom Jesus sends
to live in every believer. We need the Holy
Spirit to guide us into the full truth about Jesus
Christ. We need the Holy Spirit to direct our
steps daily, and to help us make wise choices
and godly decisions. We need the Holy Spirit to
remind us of God's commandments and the
truth of Jesus Christ so we will know what to do
and what to say in any situation in which we find
ourselves. We need the Holy Spirit to comfort us
when we experience pain and sorrow. We need
the Holy Spirit to convict us of our sins and
errors so we can repent and make positive
changes in our lives. We need the Holy Spirit
to defeat evil on our behalf. We need the Holy
Spirit to conform us to the image of Christ Jesus.
We need the Holy Spirit to make us whole.

FELLOWSHIP WITH GOD

*Truly our fellowship is with the Father
and with His Son Jesus Christ.*
1 JOHN 1:3

This is the ultimate fellowship! Knowing God. Communicating with Him—pouring out our hearts to Him and hearing His desires, His plan for us, His purposes. Loving Him with all our hearts and receiving an awareness of His vast love. Being at peace with God and knowing God's peace in our hearts. Praising God and being filled with God's joy. Being in a position to say, "*My* God." That is truly what it means to have fellowship with God.

AN INFINITE TREASURY

*His divine power has given to us all things
that pertain to life and godliness, through the knowledge
of Him who called us by glory and virtue.*

2 PETER 1:3

Many believers do not understand the vast riches they already possess in Jesus Christ, an infinite treasury of wisdom and knowledge and all good things. The moment you accept Him as your Savior you receive everything God is, everything God does, and everything God provides. You lack nothing. God's immeasurable, overflowing love and power are available to you by His grace for every trial, every decision, every challenge.

FREELY FORGIVE

If anyone has a complaint against another;
even as Christ forgave you, so you also must do.
COLOSSIANS 3:13

Forgiveness means that we are willing to let go of the pain we feel, and give it to God. We are willing to place every hurt and injustice into the hands of God and trust Him to heal our hearts and deal with those who have wounded us.

We must always forgive. There is never any situation in which unforgiveness can be justified before God. Forgiveness does not mean that we deny our injuries, dismiss our pain, or lay aside all claims to justice. It does mean that we must release that person from our own judgment and let go of any bitterness or feelings of revenge.

JESUS MEETS OUR NEEDS

Truly our fellowship is with
the Father and with His Son Jesus Christ.
1 John 1:3

Let me assure you . . .

No man can ever meet all the needs in any woman's life.

No woman can ever meet all the needs in any man's life.

No friend can ever meet all the needs in any friend's life.

But the good news is this: The Lord Jesus Christ can meet all the needs in your life so that you are better able to minister to and befriend another person.

GOD GIVES THE BEST

Whoever keeps His word,
truly the love of God is perfected in him.
1 JOHN 2:5

What is the right prayer to pray to get a marriage partner? It is this: "God, give me what I need, not what I want."

If we genuinely want what God believes that we need, then I believe God will act to give us what we need.

Too often we reject even the opportunity to get to know another person because the person isn't handsome or beautiful enough, isn't rich enough, doesn't come from the right kind of family, or doesn't have the right color of hair or the right laugh.

Be open to what God has for you. His choice will be the right one.

JESUS UNDERSTANDS

My God shall supply all your need
according to His riches in glory by Christ Jesus.
PHILIPPIANS 4:19

Jesus loves you unconditionally. His love for you is infinite and merciful. Jesus accepts you just the way you are. He never expects you to "get good" before you "get God"—to the contrary, He desires for you to receive Him so He can help you in every area of your life. . . .

Jesus understands you and cares for you. There isn't any situation in your life that is beyond His awareness, His concern, and His tender care. Jesus understands your hurts and cries with you. He shares your pain and sorrow. He never abandons you in a time of trial or suffering.

GOD SEES OUR SITUATION

The eyes of the Lord are on the righteous,
and His ears are open to their prayers.
1 PETER 3:12

Thinking about the Lord brings a person peace. Thinking about anything else is usually a shortcut to anxiety, fear, or worry.

It is important when you focus on the Lord that you see Him as being in your situation with you, right at that moment. Too many people think of God as being far away—off in heaven somewhere. Others think of God as being in their distant future—when they are older or on the brink of dying. They don't see God as being accessible or available to them in the immediacy of their lives. The truth is, He is present with us in every moment of every day.

THE FOOL'S GAME

I love those who love me,
and those who seek me diligently will find me.
PROVERBS 8:17

The fool's game is believing that "I can live my life *my way* and win." Such a life is marked by rebellion, disobedience, and pride. God simply will *not* bless or reward such a life.

You can tell me all about your degrees, experience, background, credentials, accomplishments, notoriety, fame, fortune, and awards, but if you are rejecting God in your life, you are still playing the fool's game. The most important thing you can do in your life is to receive Jesus Christ as your personal Savior.

JULY

*Our God is
great and limitless.*

COUNSEL FROM GOD'S WORD

Your testimonies also are my delight and my counselors.
PSALM 119:24

God's Word showed David which alternative to take, which option to pursue, which strategy to employ. He knew when, how, and where to apply God's Word in times of trouble. . . .

David had many counselors—brilliant and courageous "mighty men" who surrounded him with advice. But David relied first and foremost on God's Word to be his counselor. He turned first to what God had to say anytime he faced bad news or difficult circumstances. He found not only comfort but also joy in what he read and studied—he found confidence that God was with him.

UNCONDITIONAL LOVE

In this is love, not that we loved God, but that He loved us.
1 JOHN 4:10

A person can disobey God—either willfully or unknowingly—but he cannot disappoint God. A person can sin or rebel against God, and reap God's consequences for that sin as a means of chastisement. But a person cannot disappoint God.

Stop to think about it for a moment. A God who can be disappointed is a God who loves conditionally—a God who loves us when we perform well, and then withdraws His love if we perform badly. The truth of God's love is that His love is unconditional. He loves us at all times with an infinite, overwhelming, merciful, gracious, passionate love!

THE VINE AND BRANCH

I am the vine, you are the branches. He who
abides in Me, and I in him, he bears much fruit.
JOHN 15:5

Jesus makes a clear distinction between the vine
and the branch. The two are not the same.
He is the vine; we are the branches. The two are
joined but not one. The common denominator
in nature is the sap. The sap is the life of the vine
and its branches. Cut off the flow of sap to the
branch, and it slowly withers and dies.

As the branch draws its life from the vine,
so we draw life from Christ. To abide in Christ
is to draw upon His life. His life is made
available through the presence of the Holy
Spirit in our lives.

FULFILLING GOD'S PLAN

My eyes are upon You, O GOD the Lord; in You I take refuge.
PSALM 141:8

God gave you specific talents and abilities to use in fulfilling His plan and purposes for the ages. He made you to bring glory to Himself. He made you to have fellowship with Him and to be in a close, intimate relationship with Him.

I can think of no higher purpose than for a person to be a close personal friend of God and to use the talents that God has given him to the best of his ability all the days of his life. It is to this life we are called. It is for this purpose that the Holy Spirit helps and guides us on a daily basis.

NO ONE IS EXCLUDED

*Whoever believes in Him
should not perish but have everlasting life.*
JOHN 3:16

God does not parcel out salvation, deliverance, or wholeness to us bit by bit. God makes salvation completely available through Jesus Christ—and not only to specific individuals, but to all who will receive and believe in Jesus Christ as Savior.

No person is excluded from the opportunity to believe and receive everlasting life. Jesus did not say that those who believe would receive a down payment on everlasting life or a promise of everlasting life that they would have to work to fulfill. They receive everlasting life, period.

GOD IS GREAT

In quietness and confidence shall be your strength.
ISAIAH 30:15

Are you limiting God by the way you think? Imagine a circumstance that you consider bad. Use whatever descriptive words you want to use—hard, difficult, agonizing, strenuous, debilitating, horrific, sorrowful, perturbing, penetrating, or painful. Is there a problem too awful or too hard for God to handle?

If your answer to this question is anything other than "no," your understanding of God is too small.

Our God is a great and limitless God. He dwells in eternity and operates in infinity. He has all things within His understanding and all things under His control.

WALK IN WISDOM

The Spirit searches all things, yes, the deep things of God.
1 CORINTHIANS 2:10

The world says that wisdom is based upon what a person can perceive with his natural senses. God's wisdom calls for a person to walk in the discerning power of the Holy Spirit, who is not at all limited by human senses. . . .

The person who walks in godly wisdom has a "sense" or intuition provided by the Holy Spirit, who lives inside of every believer. I strongly believe that the person who functions in godly wisdom is able to see beyond what average human beings see . . . able to hear beyond what average human beings hear . . . able to understand beyond what average human beings understand. This ability flows directly from the Holy Spirit at work in us.

SUFFICIENT THROUGH GOD

*Our sufficiency is from God, who also
made us sufficient as ministers of the new covenant.*

2 CORINTHIANS 3:5–6

What good news that God is the One who makes us competent and that He is the One who makes all of our ministry efforts "sufficient."

Can you fail in witnessing to others about Christ? Not if you give your witness to the best of your ability and with a heart motivated by love.

Can you fail in praying for others in the name of Jesus? Not if you pray the way God leads you to pray and with a heart motivated by love.

Can you fail in doing a work of ministry that is designed to help others? Not if you are acting as God has led you to act and you offer your services with a heart motivated by love.

A TREMENDOUS CHALLENGE

If you keep My commandments, you will abide in My love.
JOHN 15:10

The change Jesus brings into our lives includes a tremendous challenge to become more than we presently are. Jesus is not a friend who leaves us in our weakness, winks at our sin, or allows us to continue in error. No! He accepts us where we are, but at the same time, He challenges us to move toward wholeness, perfection, and genuine excellence. He challenges us to become all that our Creator designed us to be and to do. He equips us with His presence so we can move from where we are to where He desires for us to be.

WHO'S IN CONTROL?

*Those who know Your name will put their trust
in You; for You, LORD, have not forsaken those who seek You.*
PSALM 9:10

Ask yourself "Who is in control of my material resources?" If you think you are in control, you're wrong. You certainly have a responsibility to be a good steward, or manager, of the resources God has given to you . . . but you aren't in control of your income or the material substance that comes your way. Everything you have today is a gift from God to you. He is the One who has given you the energy, vitality, health, ideas, and opportunities that have led to your "possessing" all that you have. Surely as He has provided for you all your life, He will continue to provide for you as you trust Him, obey Him, and seek to do His will.

THE HEARTBEAT OF GOD

*Every word of God is pure; He is
a shield to those who put their trust in Him.*

PROVERBS 30:5

The more we come to know God, the more we are going to learn the way God works, the things God desires to do in our lives and in the lives of others, and the plans God has made for mankind's eternal good. We are going to feel God's heartbeat. What disappoints God is going to disappoint us. What brings joy to heaven is going to bring joy to us. What brings concern to the Lord is going to concern us. We are going to see things from God's perspective, and we are going to grow in our desire to love others as God loves them.

THE POTTER'S HANDS

As the clay is in the potter's hand, so are you in My hand.
JEREMIAH 18:6

When we undergo an experience of emotional healing, it is often as if we are broken so that the Lord can completely remake us. Emotional healing is a refashioning process. The clay is still the same, the end design is still the same, but the process requires a breaking and a rebuilding so that the flaws can be removed.

Not only are we to remain steadfast, but we are to be joyful that God is at work in our lives. We are to thank Him daily that He is healing us, restoring us, and making us whole. We are who we are, each one of us, because the Lord is making us who we are. We are His workmanship.

GOD'S NEVER-ENDING LOVE

We love Him because He first loved us.
1 JOHN 4:19

God's love is flowing toward each one of us as a deep, wide, beautiful, and never-ending river. It is up to us to jump in.

God's love is also unconditional. It is not based upon what we do, what we have, or what we achieve. His love is given to us because of who we are, His creation. It is not grounded on any other premise or motivation.

You can't earn unconditional love. You can't merit it in any way. You can't deserve it. God says you are worthy of His love solely because it is His desire to love you. There is nothing you can do to win more of God's love.

NOBLE THOUGHTS

Commit your works to the LORD,
and your thoughts will be established.

PROVERBS 16:3

The noblest thoughts you can produce are thoughts about God.

Think about how God has been faithful to you in giving you so many good things— far more good things than you can number!

Think about the plans and purposes God has for you throughout all eternity. Think about the heavenly home He is preparing for you. You can never fully exhaust your ability to think about the goodness and greatness of God. You will never reach the end of your praise to Him.

LOVING AS WE ARE LOVED

You shall love your neighbor as yourself.
MATTHEW 22:39

We are to love our neighbors as God loves them just as we love ourselves as God loves us. When we factor God's love into the equation, everything becomes crystal clear! To love others in a genuine, sacrificial, and pure way, we must know what it means to be loved.

We see the evidence of such love best in the life and death of Jesus Christ. Jesus genuinely loved those who followed Him. . . . Jesus' love was unconditional. It is only as we receive such love into our lives and acknowledge the importance that God places upon us as individuals beloved by Him that we truly can give such love to others and fully appreciate the importance that God places upon them.

SERVING WITH JOY

The manifestation of the Spirit
is given to each one for the profit of all.
1 CORINTHIANS 12:7

When we minister to others through our gifts, we are tapping in to the inexhaustible energy and motivation of God. When we exercise our gifts, the Holy Spirit flows through us like at no other time. We are doing what we have been called and equipped to do. We experience an extra measure of energy and joy.

Serving outside our gifts is a different story altogether. I believe this is the primary reason so many Christians get burned out on church work. Instead of finding a slot where they can use their gifts, they sign up for whatever opening there is at the time. They do their best as long as they can take it, then they quit.

OBEYING GOD'S COMMANDS

You shall not commit adultery.
MATTHEW 19:18

Every one of God's commands related to other people exists so that both you and the other person will be in a position to avoid harm. God's command, "You shall not commit adultery," was given so that *your* heart might not be broken, *your* marriage might not be destroyed, *your* reputation might not be damaged, *your* future might not be impaired, and *your* standing of innocence and purity before God might not be tainted. The commandment, when kept, yields a benefit to others and to society as a whole, but the primary beneficiary in keeping the commandment is the person who keeps it.

TRUE HOPE

This hope we have as an anchor
of the soul, both sure and steadfast.
HEBREWS 6:19

So many people I know live under a terrible cloud of "I hope I've done enough to please God." They hope they've read enough of the Bible and prayed enough. They hope God will forgive them. They hope they'll be considered worthy of heaven.

Such concern isn't true hope.

True hope lies in saying, "Thank You, God, for saving me! Thank You for loving me! Thank You for Jesus Christ and what He did for me on the cross! Thank You for giving me Your Holy Spirit to guide me and comfort me!"

SALVATION

Unless one is born of water and the Spirit, he cannot enter the kingdom of God. . . . You must be born again.
JOHN 3:5, 7

Every person needs to be cleansed from sin. Every person needs to be released from the burden of guilt, filled with the Holy Spirit, and made whole spiritually.

So many falsehoods are circulating today about how a person comes to be a Christian. Let me state it very plainly for you:

Salvation isn't gained by being good.

Salvation isn't gained by doing good. . . .

Salvation is gained by receiving Christ into your life and dwelling in Him even as He dwells in you.

HEARING AND OBEYING

I will delight in Your statutes; I will not forget Your word.
PSALM 119:16

To walk wisely, we must actively and diligently obey and apply God's Word to our lives. It's not enough to hear God's Word, to read it, or to meditate on it. We must do it. . . .

Those who are willing to obey God's Word are going to be the ones who are most clearly and directly impacted by God's Word. They have set their minds and hearts to know God's Word. They read God's Word with the thought: *I've got to see what God wants me to do. I'm going to discover today some of the ways God wants me to live and respond and initiate action. I'm reading my Bible for guidance for my life, not just to have something good to read for my mind.*

TODAY AND TOMORROW

*The counsel of the LORD
stands forever; the plans of His heart to all generations.*
PSALM 33:11

A person may say:
"Suppose I don't get into the college of my choice . . ."

"Suppose I don't get the job I want . . ."

"Suppose the person I love doesn't love me back . . ."

Friend, the God who is in control of today is also the God who is fully in control of tomorrow. He has already prepared for what will happen to you! He has already provided what you will need tomorrow. He has already anticipated the problems you will face tomorrow and has set into motion everything required to resolve those problems.

SIMPLY TRUSTING

To You, O LORD, I lift up my soul. O my God, I trust in You.
PSALM 25:1–2

We are called by God to trust Him, and Him alone, to meet our needs and to be our total source of supply. Furthermore, God requires that we obey Him as a part of our trusting Him. We have the situation completely backward anytime we start expecting God to trust us to know what is right and to obey our commands so that He might prove His love for us.

Our position is one of standing before God, declaring, "I trust You completely to meet my needs in Your timing and according to Your methods." Anyone who takes the stance before almighty God, "You must do things *my* way," is presumptuous and foolish.

DISCOVERING GOD'S WILL

Teach me Your way, O LORD; I will walk in Your truth.
PSALM 86:11

The Holy Spirit speaks to neutral hearts. By that, I don't mean passive or indifferent hearts. God gave us the ability to dream dreams and make plans. Many of the Old and New Testament leaders were men and women of vision and ambition.

By neutral, I mean being consumed with discovering what pleases the Holy Spirit rather than working to convince Him of the wisdom and brilliance of our plans. I'm afraid many of us pray with the goal of talking God into things rather than trying to discover His will. As a result, we never hear Him.

THE BIG PICTURE

Put on the whole armor of God, that you
may be able to stand against the wiles of the devil.
EPHESIANS 6:11

If I am out in the snowcapped mountains on a photography trip, I have a number of options. I can use a wide-angle lens to take in the full panorama of a mountain ridge. Or I can put a longer lens on my camera and focus on one aspect of a mountain.

The same happens in a temptation to sin. When we focus only on what we need in a given moment, we lose all sense of the big picture of our lives. We shut out all thoughts of penalty for sin, and we focus only on the pleasure we believe we will experience. In order to build a defense against this tactic of the devil, we need to keep the big picture of our lives always before us.

WE WORK WITH GOD

The steps of a good man are ordered
by the LORD, and He delights in his way.
PSALM 37:23

In the Gospel of John, Jesus described the Holy Spirit as our Helper, our Counselor, our Advocate. He is not described as the One who will do everything for us and require nothing of us.

An older farmer gave this advice to a younger farmer: "Ask God to show you what to plant and when to plant. Then plant the best seed you can buy. Ask God to grow the seeds. Then cultivate the ground, pull the weeds, and fertilize the plants as they grow. Ask God to produce a great harvest. Then go out and gather the harvest when it is ripe. Ask God to show you how to market your produce. Then take your produce to market. Don't try to do God's part. And don't expect God to do yours."

GOD'S MASTERPIECE

We are His workmanship,
created in Christ Jesus for good works.
EPHESIANS 2:10

Although God cares about financial stability, world peace, and social justice, He has one great thing on His mind today—you. You are His workmanship, His masterpiece. There is no one else exactly like you, and God cares for you with infinite watchfulness. He knows exactly how many hairs came out in your brush this morning. Your checkbook matters as much as the federal budget, harmony in your home as much as harmony among nations.

LOVE WITHOUT LIMITS

Love . . . bears all things,
believes all things, hopes all things, endures all things.
1 CORINTHIANS 13:4, 7

Don't tell me that you love another person,
but you are unwilling to talk to that person.
Don't tell me that you love another person, but
you just can't open up and be transparent about
your feelings, ideas, or your past experiences.
Don't tell me that you love another person,
but you are unwilling to work on getting to the
core issue of a problem that exists between you.
. . . Genuine love never limits conversation,
transparency, or personal self-examination.
Genuine love is marked by generous giving and
a willingness to change, grow, mature, and share
the fullness of life with another person.

GODLY RELATIONSHIPS

Be kindly affectionate to one another with
brotherly love, in honor giving preference to one another.
ROMANS 12:10

Godly relationships are those in which there is a willingness to say, "I don't have to have things my way all the time. I'm willing to submit my desires to your desires, my preferences to your preferences." Certainly we are never called to compromise our values, our faith in Christ Jesus, or with evil. We also are never to give up our entire identity just to please another person or to become a doormat on which he walks. We are, however, to mature to the point that we are more concerned about what happens to another person than we are concerned about what happens to us. We are willing to allow our friends the freedom of expression, and we are willing to value their choices, their ideas, and their desires.

EVERY MINUTE OF THE DAY

Lo, I am with you always, even to the end of the age.
MATTHEW 28:20

In the form of the Holy Spirit, Jesus is with us at all times. He is *always* present in our lives, every minute of every hour of every day.

How blessed we are to live in the time of the Holy Spirit! When Jesus was alive on the earth, He could not be in two places at one time. But now, Jesus is free of all constraints of time and space. By the power of the Holy Spirit, He is with each of those who believe in Him at all times. We never need to call for Jesus to show up. He is already present.

GOD IS OUR DEFENSE

Though war may rise against me, in this I will be confident.
PSALM 27:3

These are the words of a man who has learned how to be sustained in the most difficult, trying times of life. He learned an amazing lesson—in the midst of tragedy, he did not need to live in fear, because God was his defense. Though in a war zone, he could be fully confident that God would protect and sustain him

There is hope for us because God has promised never to leave us or to forsake us. There is hope because we are not alone— we have each other. This is the strength of a nation under attack—a united spirit gaining confidence and determination from each other. But more importantly, learning to rely on our God.

THE DEPTH OF HIS LOVE

Come to Me, all you who labor
and are heavy laden, and I will give you rest.
MATTHEW 11:28

Jesus has time for you. He is never too busy for you. He will listen to you, no matter what you desire to say to Him. Jesus has answers for you. No matter what problem or difficulty you are facing, Jesus has a way out of your negative situation. He will speak to you through His Word and through the Holy Spirit prompting you to take godly actions. Jesus not only gives us answers about life, but He readily reveals to us Himself. He is quick to show us how He works, what He desires, how much He loves, and the depth of His concern. He will answer any question you ever have about who He is.

AUGUST

*God desires
to live with you forever.*

WHAT DOES GOD SAY?

Oh, how I love Your law! It is my meditation all the day.
PSALM 119:97

Anytime we face an issue that we know is truly important, we need to go to the Word of God to find out what God says on the matter. God has not left out any topic—He has left no void regarding those things that are most important in life. The Bible is God's viewpoint; it is His opinion, His counsel, and His advice. . . .

God's commandments, statutes, precepts, and principles cover all of life's situations. We need to ponder God's Word—read it, study it, memorize it, think about it, and consider it. In doing so, we discover the wise way to handle life and to respond to the difficult situations we all face.

GOD-GIVEN GOALS

*No good thing will He
withhold from those who walk uprightly.*
PSALM 84:11

God will not lead you into unrealistic thinking. . . .

I didn't say the Lord wouldn't challenge you to do what seems impossible to you. I said He wouldn't lead you into something that was unrealistic.

The "impossible goals" that the Lord lays before us are goals that are in keeping with the talents and abilities He has given us. They are things that we cannot achieve apart from the use of our faith. There is a dimension to these goals that is God's realm. Only He can cause all the pieces to fall into place. Only He can cause the seeds of time, effort, and skill associated with the goal to come to full fruition.

SURRENDER

*God resists the proud, but gives grace
to the humble. Therefore submit to God.*
JAMES 4:6–7

As long as a drowning man thinks he can help himself, he is dangerous to anyone who tries to help him. His tendency is to grab the one trying to aid him and take them both down in the process. The correct procedure is to stay just far enough away so that he can't grab you. Then you wait. And when he finally gives up, you make your move. At that point the one drowning is pliable. He won't work against you. He will let you help.

The same principle holds true in our relationship with the Holy Spirit. Until we give up, we aren't really in a position to be helped. We will work against Him rather than with Him. Surrender to His will follows the surrender of our own.

GOD'S CHILDREN

The Spirit Himself bears witness with our spirit
that we are children of God, and if children, then heirs.
ROMANS 8:16–17

Regardless of the circumstances of your birth or the experiences of your childhood; regardless of your human parents or your social status; regardless of your race, sex, cultural background, or physical appearance; regardless of what others say about you or how they treat you; regardless of anything external or historical about you; you can know that you belong fully to God's family. You are His child!

What good news this is! We do not have to do anything to win our way into the arms of our heavenly Father. We do not have to achieve anything before we enter His presence. He makes Himself totally and completely available to us.

THE RICHES OF HIS GLORY

Of His fullness we have all received, and grace for grace.
JOHN 1:16

The grace of God at work in our lives unfolds to us as we are able to experience it. All of God's gifts are deposited into our spiritual account, but as we grow in Christ, we have the ability to access the riches of His glory. It is as if the fullness of God's gifts to us has been put in a trust account on our behalf—just as a parent might set up a trust fund for a child, a fund the child cannot access or spend until he has reached a certain age. The Lord knows not only what we need, but also what we are able to handle.

GOD KNOWS EVERYTHING

*Look at the birds of the air, for they neither
sow nor reap . . . yet your heavenly Father feeds them.*
MATTHEW 6:26

The key to overcoming anxiety is to get your thinking right about God. The fact is, God is sovereign. He created everything and has absolute control over every aspect of His creation. He is all-powerful, all-knowing, and ever present.

He knows absolutely everything about your situation. He knows how to produce wholeness out of brokenness. He knows how to build strength out of weakness. He knows how to heal what is sick. He knows how to bring reconciliation and love out of estrangement and hate.

He loves you with an unconditional, unfathomable, immeasurable love.

GOD'S INFINITE WISDOM

The way of life winds upward for the wise.
PROVERBS 15:24

Earthly wisdom is limited. It generally is
based upon the best that collective humanity
has been able to conclude or to decipher. . . .

God's wisdom, in contrast, is unlimited.
It is based upon what God sees when He looks
to ages past and ahead to ages still to come. It is
based upon the whole of any given life or
situation. Godly wisdom says, "This is the way I
made man to act, respond, and succeed." Godly
wisdom concludes, "This is what God wants."

If we want to be wise, we must choose to
see things from God's perspective.

BY GOD'S SPIRIT

"Not by might nor by power,
but by My Spirit," says the LORD *of hosts.*
ZECHARIAH 4:6

We are not equipped to fulfill God's plan for our lives in our own strength. God has given us talents and abilities, and He has given us the Holy Spirit to enable and empower us to use our talents and abilities effectively. . . .

As competent as we may become in our own strength, we are never as fully competent by ourselves as we can be if we will allow the Holy Spirit to work in us and through us to accomplish God's will for us. Our competency may be great, but it is never complete until we allow the Holy Spirit to enlarge, enhance, multiply, and bless our efforts.

OUR PROVIDER

It is He who has made us, and not
we ourselves; we are His people and the sheep of His pasture.
PSALM 100:3

If you doubt God's ability to provide for you, remind yourself of the many methods He has used to provide for His people. Remember as you read about His provision that God is the same today as He was in Bible times. His nature as your Provider is unwavering. His resources are unlimited. His love for you is infinite. And His power to provide is absolute.

You cannot have peace and at the same time doubt that God will provide for you. Settle the issue once and for all in your heart and mind. God is your Provider. He will meet your needs as you learn to trust and obey Him.

DISCERNMENT

*I have taught you in the way
of wisdom; I have led you in right paths.*
PROVERBS 4:11

God sees the totality of your life. He knows you inside and out. He knows your thoughts, your feelings, your physical makeup. He knows your past, your present, and your future. He knows your natural talents, your experiences, your spiritual gifts. God sees the whole of who you are, what you are called to do, and what you are facing right now. The more you see your life from God's perspective, the stronger your ability to discern the right way to go. . . .

There is nobody better qualified than God to guide your steps or to lead you into right paths.

THREE ANSWERS

The grace of God that brings salvation has appeared . . .
teaching us that . . .we should live soberly, righteously.
TITUS 2:11–12

"Why am I here? Why did God create me?" Perhaps you have asked these questions yourself. The answer at its most basic level is threefold:

1. You were created for an intimate fellowship with God and to have daily communication with Him.
2. You were created to overcome evil and establish God's goodness on this earth.
3. You were created to have close relationships with others so that you might have companionship, friendship, and assistance as you praise and worship God, and do the work God has put before you to do.

GOD'S PURPOSE AND PLAN

I have set before you an open door, and no one can shut it.
REVELATION 3:8

God's purpose is that you receive His love, and then express His love to others. God desires to be in personal relationship with you so you might experience His love on a daily basis.

God's master plan for you is the acceptance of Jesus Christ as your Savior so you might receive His ongoing grace in this life and His gift of eternal life in heaven. God desires to live with you forever. Heaven is your destiny— yes, it's your ultimate destination. His plan is always one that brings you to wholeness and the receiving of all things designed for your eternal good. What a wonderful destiny that is!

RENEW YOUR MIND

Do not be conformed to this world,
but be transformed by the renewing of your mind.
ROMANS 12:2

Most of us are not what we think we are. Our thinking is marred and needs to be changed.

How do I know this to be true? Not only by the many people with whom I have had contact through the years, but also from God's Word. The Bible calls us to a "renewal" of our minds. That means change. That means trading in our old perceptions, old opinions, old ideas, old beliefs, and old self-centered attitudes on a new set of perceptions, opinions, ideas, beliefs, and attitudes that God develops in us.

AVOIDING EVIL

Do not be overcome by evil, but overcome evil with good.
ROMANS 12:21

God gave Adam and Eve His presence, each other, and total material and natural provision with one stipulation: do not engage in what will result in your knowing evil and experiencing its deadly consequences.

God gives us as His children today His presence through the Holy Spirit, one another in the form of the body of Christ (the church as a whole), and a promise of total material and natural provision with one stipulation: do not engage in what will result in your knowing evil and experiencing its deadly consequences.

We are to be aware of evil and to avoid it. We are to be wise to the tactics of Satan to tempt us to engage in evil and we are to be bold in saying no to him.

LIVING GOD'S WILL

As many as are led by the
Spirit of God, these are sons of God.
ROMANS 8:14

I learned a long time ago that one sure way to get a crowd is to announce you are going to speak on the topic "How to Find the Will of God." People want three easy steps to know God's will for their lives—His personal will, that is. On the other hand, announce that your topic will be "God's Plan for Holy Living," and you will be lucky if anybody shows up.

The Holy Spirit does aid the believer in discovering God's personal will. But His primary role as a leader and guide is to lead the believer into holiness.

PHYSICAL HEALTH

A sound heart is life to the body.
PROVERBS 14:30

God's command for us to love ourselves means, in part, that we are to do nothing that will bring harm to ourselves. We will take no substance into our bodies that is known to cause bodily harm or mental deficiency. We will engage in no activities that we know will bring detriment to us. We will forge no alliances or relationships that we know will be hurtful to us financially, materially, physically, or emotionally. God gave His law to mankind not to diminish man's fun or to put a damper on man's ability to experience life fully; rather, He gave the law so that man might avoid circumstances that would produce physical, material, emotional, or spiritual harm.

DEEP SATISFACTION

I have loved you with an everlasting love;
therefore with lovingkindness I have drawn you.
JEREMIAH 31:3

The person who accepts God's love experiences a deep-seated satisfaction that no matter what happens, God is present. The person who accepts God's love invariably must accept God's provision for forgiveness—Jesus Christ crucified and resurrected. That is the only means that God has provided for you truly to feel deep satisfaction that your spirit has been cleansed and renewed. Unless you know that you are forgiven, you cannot know the satisfaction of feeling safe from the assaults of the devil, the satisfaction of feeling free from the weight of guilt and sin, the satisfaction of knowing that God has provided an eternal home for you.

WE NEED GOD'S LOVE

There is none upon earth that I desire besides You.
PSALM 73:25

The person who has a need for intimacy feels estranged, cut off, separated, unfulfilled. These feelings are defined as sexual desire, but they are really symptoms of a need to be loved in a way that is comforting, consistent, and unconditional. Only God can provide this kind of love in its purest and richest form. People often use phrases such as "if I could only be held by someone" or "if I only had someone who really knew me and really loved me completely" to express the root need, "I need to be embraced by someone who will never let go of me and never stop loving me." That Someone is God.

SWEETER THAN HONEY

How sweet are Your words
to my taste, sweeter than honey to my mouth!
PSALM 119:103

King David spent a lot of time reading, studying, and thinking about God's Word. He delighted in his study and reflection on God's principles. He not only committed God's Word to his memory, but he frequently recalled God's Word and steeped his thinking in God's law. He did not forget God's Word when it came time for him to speak, to act, or to compose songs. Rather, what he had been thinking about became his speech, his lyrics, and his motivation for behavior. He reflected God's Word in the judgments he made.

God's Word was "sweet" to David—in fact, he said it was sweeter than honey—because the end result of applying God's Word was pleasant, beneficial, and good.

FOUNDATION OF FAITH

Having been justified by faith, we have peace with God.
ROMANS 5:1

There is only one way to experience an abiding peace that transcends circumstances. The answer is "by faith." By faith we ask and then trust God to be present in our lives. It is as though we have put a sum of money in the bank, and by faith we write checks because we know that there are funds already deposited to cover our withdrawals. We have asked God to accept and forgive us and to be present in our lives with His abiding peace, and then we go out and live expecting Him to do the very thing we trust Him to do.

The foundation for living in God's peace is faith.

CONFORMED TO CHRIST

Bear one another's burdens, and so fulfill the law of Christ.
GALATIANS 6:2

One area in which God always challenges us to grow and change is in our character. The Bible tells us that God is at work in every believer's life to conform that person into the character likeness of Christ Jesus. . . .

Everyone can always be more loving. Everyone can always have still greater joy, be more at peace, have greater patience, show more kindness, reflect more goodness, walk in greater faithfulness. They can express themselves with greater gentleness, and manifest more self-control. No matter how mature the believer, there's always room for growth in these areas.

YOUR KINGDOM NICHE

He fashions their hearts individually;
He considers all their works.

PSALM 33:15

God has a kingdom niche carved out just for you. There are people He wants you to meet, lives He wants you to influence. He is tailoring your personality in such a way that you will hit it off with unsaved men and women who otherwise would never have the opportunity to experience a relationship with a believer. You are the instrument God wants to use to change someone's distorted perception of Christianity. You will be the one God uses to reshape someone's thinking and thereby prepare the way for salvation. That is, if you are willing to make the discovery of His will your priority.

MEETING YOUR NEEDS

God is faithful, who will not allow
you to be tempted beyond what you are able.
1 CORINTHIANS 10:13

A temptation always strikes at an area of need we perceive—it may be a need for higher self-value, attention, appreciation, or approval; a need for love and affection; a need that is physical or sexual; or a need rooted in loneliness or pride, among others. Ask yourself immediately in the face of temptation, "Is there another way—a good way, a right way—of getting this need met in my life?" The answer is always "yes." God always has a godly alternative for meeting the deep needs of your life. He wants you to have His wisdom about how to meet your deepest emotional needs.

STRONG IN HIS STRENGTH

I will rather boast in my infirmities,
that the power of Christ may rest upon me. . . . For when
I am weak, then I am strong.
2 CORINTHIANS 12:9–10

Paul's thorn-in-the-flesh experience brought him to the position where he could fully allow the strength of Christ to be his strength. . . .

Some people today will claim, "Troubles make you strong." They are wrong. Troubles destroy some people. Troubles weaken others. There is nothing inherent about troubles that results in making us strong emotionally and spiritually. The truth, as Paul stated it so well, is that when we rely upon Christ Jesus in our times of trouble, *He* makes us strong. He imparts His strength to us and as we receive His strength, we are made strong.

WATCH AND WAIT

Commit your way to the LORD,
trust also in Him, and He shall bring it to pass.
PSALM 37:5

At times, God requires a season of waiting before He sends His blessing. Then trust becomes your greatest asset. If you don't trust God with your need, you will cry out in fear and panic. At one point during a storm on the Sea of Galilee, the disciples thought they would perish. But Jesus commanded the wind and waves to be still. He taught those men how to trust Him even in the most tempestuous of circumstances, and He is teaching you to watch and wait for His outstretched arm.

SHOWING KINDNESS

If your enemy is hungry,
feed him; if he is thirsty, give him a drink.
ROMANS 12:20

In Bible times, to give food and water to a hungry, thirsty enemy was a sign of tremendous hospitality. People knew that if you turned a hungry, thirsty enemy away from your tent out into the wilderness, that enemy would only seek to do you more harm. Showing basic kindness to the enemy, on the other hand, was a means of defusing his anger and possibly putting a stop to his evil actions. . . .

There's nothing in the Bible that states we are to go out of our way to make extravagant gestures of generosity to those who do evil to us. . . . What we are required by God to do is to meet their basic human needs if and when those needs present themselves. We are to be courteous to them, speak kindly to them, and refuse to criticize them.

CHARLES STANLEY   255

CONSTRUCTIVE ANGER

Be angry and do not sin.
EPHESIANS 4:26

There is a way to express anger "without sinning." We can channel our anger into constructive change—putting the focus on what we can and should do rather than on what we want the other person to do. We can address concerns and problems before they fester to the boiling point. We can share our frustrations and feelings before bitterness or hate reaches the explosion level. We can voice that we are upset, concerned, disappointed, or in pain without raising our voice, digging up the past, or ripping apart another person's identity. And we can always choose to give voice to our emotions without striking out at a person's personal characteristics—appearance, desirability, race, age, cultural background, family upbringing, or character faults.

TEMPTATION AND ERROR

*Each one is tempted when he is
drawn away by his own desires and enticed.*

JAMES 1:14

What exactly is temptation? It is an enticement to get a legitimate need met apart from God's will or outside God's boundaries.

Some people feel guilty for having needs. That is false guilt. Needs are needs. . . . Needs are legitimate, and all of our needs are worthy of bringing to Christ so that He might meet them. Don't feel guilty for having needs.

Guilt arises—and should arise—when we attempt to meet our needs by our manipulation or efforts rather than by trust in God.

AUGUST 29

FORGIVE THE DEBT

Forgive us our debts, as we forgive our debtors.
MATTHEW 6:12

Forgiveness is the act of setting someone free
from an obligation to you that is a result of
a wrong done against you. For example, a debt
is forgiven when you free your debtor of his
obligation to pay back what he owes you.

Forgiveness, then, involves three elements:
injury, a *debt* resulting from the injury, and a
cancellation of the debt. All three elements are
essential if forgiveness is to take place.

RECEIVE AND ACCEPT

By grace you have been saved through faith,
and that not of yourselves; it is the gift of God, not of works.
EPHESIANS 2:8–9

Jesus chose us while we were sinners. He chose us so He might save us, heal us, restore us to a right relationship with the Father, and walk with us in intimate friendship the rest of our lives. . . .

Our friendship with God is the result of nothing that we have done or can ever do. We must be willing to lay down our pride and humbly receive what He has done on our behalf. We must accept His death on the cross as being on our behalf. We must receive His indwelling presence in the form of the Holy Spirit. We must gratefully acknowledge that He is the One who paid the price in full for our friendship with God.

OVERFLOWING GENEROSITY

A faithful man will abound with blessings.
PROVERBS 28:20

S how me a person who is overflowing in generosity to another person, and I'll show you a person rich in friendships.

Show me a person who is extremely generous in the giving of her time to other people, and I'll show you a person who always has people "there" for her in times of her need.

Show me a person who can't give enough of himself to further the specific ministry calling that God has placed on his life, and I'll show you a person who has a tremendous sense of purpose and fulfillment.

SEPTEMBER

All truth points to God.

WHOLE IN GOD'S EYES

Teach me to do Your will, for You are my God.
PSALM 143:10

Wholeness from God's perspective is to be complete; to know with deep assurance that we are beloved by God with an everlasting, infinite, and unconditional love; to be able to move forward with boldness and confidence that we are God's children; to claim God's promises that we are victors through Christ Jesus over every negative situation and circumstance; and to be able to stand up to the enemy of our souls regardless of what the devil may throw at us.

Wholeness is the work that God does in us with a twofold purpose: that we might be sound in spirit, mind, and emotions, and that we might influence others to accept God's love, forgiveness, and plan.

PRAISE AND FAITH

The voice of rejoicing and
salvation is in the tents of the righteous.
PSALM 118:15

Our petitions, thanksgiving, and praise must all be bathed by our faith. We must truly believe that God is capable and is in control of all things. We must truly believe that God desires our eternal good. We must truly believe that God is our help in time of need.

When we catch even a glimpse of who God is, what God is capable of doing, and how He desires to exert the full extent of His power, presence, and provision to help us, we can't help but feel faith and hope welling up in us to produce an abiding peace.

FAITH IS BELIEVING

As you therefore have received
Christ Jesus the Lord, so walk in him.
COLOSSIANS 2:6

Faith is believing that God will do as He has promised. Faith is not a power. It's not something we are supposed to drum up inside ourselves. Faith is trusting that God will honor His promises. That is all there is to it.

Our part in the faith process is fairly simple. We are to go about our lives—making decisions, handling crises, raising our families, and so on—as if God is really going to do what He said He would do. That is what it means to walk by faith. . . .

The Holy Spirit dwells in you and is ready to go to work producing the character of Christ through you. All He needs is your faith.

ENCOURAGING OTHERS

*If I will that he remain till
I come, what is that to you? You follow Me.*
JOHN 21:22

The Lord has a plan for each of us, and it is our responsibility to live out that plan in obedience and faithfulness. What the Lord plans for another person's life—and how that other person lives out God's plan—is the business only of the Lord and that person. It is not our responsibility. We are to encourage and help others as they fulfill God's plan in their lives, but we are not the creator, originator, manipulator, or policeman of that plan and purpose. God is fully capable of dealing with each person individually, and our role is to trust Him completely with our lives and with the lives of those we love.

OUR DAILY BREAD

Give us this day our daily bread.
MATTHEW 6:11

Jesus taught His disciples to pray, "Our Father in heaven . . . give us this day our daily bread." The concept of daily bread goes far beyond a loaf of whole wheat bread for physical nourishment. *Bread* is a term that refers to everything that is necessary for wholeness in life. It refers to the things we need physically, but also to the things we need mentally, emotionally, and spiritually. . . .

When you ask the Lord to give you your daily bread, you are also to mean, "Give me today what You know I need to carry out Your purposes for me on the earth. I trust You to meet all my needs."

SAFE WITH THE SHEPHERD

I am the door of the sheep. . . . If anyone enters by Me,
he will be saved, and will go in and out and find pasture.
JOHN 10:7

In this verse, Jesus was referring to the fact that in Bible times, shepherds slept with their sheep when the sheep spent the night in outdoor pens that were made of rocks. The shepherd would lie in the open doorway that allowed the sheep to enter the pen. With his very life, the shepherd would protect the sheep from any predators or thieves. Note that Jesus said that we are not only saved because Jesus stands between us and the enemy who seeks to steal, kill, and destroy us, but that Jesus, as our Shepherd, allows us to "find pasture." That little two-word phrase means that a sheep has all of its needs for survival met fully.

WISE DECISIONS

Happy is the man who finds wisdom,
and the man who gains understanding.
PROVERBS 3:13

We are called to be wise in every decision of our lives. We need God's wisdom in our business dealings, our health, our relationships, our parenting, our finances, and our relationship with Him. No area of life is beyond the need for wisdom, off-limits to God's wisdom, or ignored by God's Word. God's wisdom can be readily applied to every decision or choice we make, every relationship we have, every emotion we feel, every action we take, every opinion we hold, and every idea or challenge we pursue.

PERFECTION IS IMPOSSIBLE

Having been justified by faith, we have peace with God.
ROMANS 5:1

To strive for perfection is futile.

"Well, should I just give up trying?" you may ask.

Trying to do your best? No, never give up on that.

Trying to *be* the best at all times? Trying to live an error-free life? Yes. Give it up.

Trying to do it in your own strength and power? Trying to force others to serve you and make you number one? Yes. Give it up.

Trying to live your life without God's help? Most definitely, yes, give it up.

THE SOURCE
OF OUR STRENGTH

I can do all things through Christ who strengthens me.
PHILIPPIANS 4:13

Anytime you feel inadequate, go to God and say, "I feel inadequate. I'm trusting You to be my adequacy."

If you feel ignorant, trust God to be your source of wisdom.

If you feel weak or exhausted, trust God to be your strength.

If you feel yourself totally without adequate resources, trust God to provide what you need.

LOVER OF MY SOUL

Whoever finds [wisdom]
finds life, and obtains favor from the LORD.
PROVERBS 8:35

If you truly believe you are associated with
God who reveals Himself to you, guides you
daily, protects you always, gives you strength
and power to make it through every day with
hope and courage, and imparts to you joy and
contentment, how can you have a poor self-
image? The almighty, awesome God of the
universe is your heavenly Father! He is not only
your Creator but also your Sustainer, Provider,
Protector, and Lover of your soul forever. You are
His child, and you will live with Him forever.

How can a poor self-image thrive in the face
of such beliefs?

GOD NEVER CHANGES

*How precious also are Your thoughts
to me, O God! How great is the sum of them!*
PSALM 139:17

Many experts believe that because of the 9/11 attacks, life and the way we do some things may never be the same again. But of this you can be certain. No matter what transpires to change your circumstances, your heavenly Father will always be the same! He is not thrown by tragedy. The eternal God will walk with you the rest of your life. He will help you. Further, if you so choose, He will enable you to live life more fully than you have before.

SINGLE-MINDED PURSUIT

You will seek the LORD your God, and you will find Him if you seek Him with all your heart and with all your soul.
DEUTERONOMY 4:29

To seek God means to pursue Him as life's only definitive and ultimate source for meaning and truth, for understanding and wisdom. It means to consult God first and foremost in all matters.

When we seek God, of course, we seek His commandments, His righteousness, His purity, His statutes—all of the attributes and manifestations of His being. God cannot be separated from His goodness, His justice, His provision. To seek God is to seek His way for living a life that is pleasing to Him.

TRUTH AND FACTS

When He, the Spirit of truth,
has come, He will guide you into all truth.
JOHN 16:13

There is a big difference between facts and truth. Facts are rooted in details that tell who, what, when, where, and how. Truth, however, encompasses more than facts. It is rooted in *significance* and *meaning*. You can know the facts of an event or situation or experience, but only as you understand the meaning of the significance of what has happened can you come to know the truth. Ultimately, truth has an eternal, divine quality to it. All truth flows from God. All truth points to God. Your quest must be not to get only the facts in life, but to understand life's facts in the context of God's truth that has eternal purposes.

THE WORK OF THE SPIRIT

The Holy Spirit, . . . will teach you all things.
JOHN 14:26

It is the Holy Spirit who works in us to
- prick our consciences if we are about to sin or have made a choice or decision that is going to lead us astray from God's perfect will for our lives.
- enable us to withstand and say no to a temptation.
- convict us of sin that we commit so we will turn immediately to the Lord and seek forgiveness.
- show us the choices we are to make and the opportunities we are to pursue.

A CHILD OF THE KING!

The LORD is our King; He will save us.
ISAIAH 33:22

God has given us a healthy way to love
ourselves. The word that most readily
comes to mind is *respect*. Respect yourself.
That is what it means to have good self-value or
self-worth. Regard yourself as God regards you—
a unique, irreplaceable, and beloved creation
with a divine and eternal plan and purpose.

Don't allow what others say to drag you down.
Don't put yourself down.

Hold your head up and face the world with
the knowledge that you are a child of God and
your Father is the King of the universe!

WALKING IN THE SPIRIT

Walk in the Spirit, and you
shall not fulfill the lust of the flesh.
GALATIANS 5:16

The immediate result of walking by the Spirit is not discovering which job to take, which person to marry, or which car to buy. The immediate result is that you will not carry out the desires of the flesh. To do one is not to do the other. Paul does more than command us not to fulfill the desires of the flesh. The command is to live in dependency on and sensitive to the prompting of the Holy Spirit. Saying no to the desires of the flesh will be the natural outcome of walking in the Spirit.

MADE WHOLE

The young lions lack and suffer hunger;
but those who seek the LORD shall not lack any good thing.
PSALM 34:10

God sees your whole life, and He views your life as a whole. You cannot divide your life into compartments and say, "This is my spiritual life and this is my material life and this is my home life and this is my financial life." Your life functions as a whole. And the whole of you is in Christ when you become a Christian. Christ is involved in every area of your life. He makes you whole; He does not divide you or separate the areas of your life one from another. This means, of course, that Christ Jesus is involved in every aspect of your neediness. He is concerned not only with your spiritual neediness, but also with your financial, material, physical, relational, and emotional needs.

OUR POTENTIAL IS VAST

I will run the course of Your
commandments, for You shall enlarge my heart.
PSALM 119:32

God has given us a great potential. Our potential is vast—so much greater than most of us know. The majority of people never even stop to think about potential, and those who do usually estimate the potential as being much less than it actually is. As a result, we shortchange ourselves, achieve less, and fail to dream big enough dreams.

God is infinite, and when He pours Himself into us and into our abilities, we take on His capacity, not our capacity. When God pours Himself into the tasks that He calls us to do, there is no limit to how much He can multiply our efforts to accomplish His purposes.

TRUE LOVE

The God of love and peace will be with you.
2 CORINTHIANS 13:11

Two people may love each other the best they know how to love, but genuine unconditional love—love that gives and gives and gives without recrimination or any tinge of retribution—is divine.

When a person turns to God and seeks to build a relationship with God, when a person receives God's forgiveness and love, when a person spends time with God, shares his heart fully and honestly with God, and engages in frequent and in-depth conversations with God, such a person knows truly what it means to be in an intimate relationship. Once a person knows that, it is so much more meaningful, and so much easier, to develop an intimate relationship with another person.

CAPTAIN OF OUR SOULS

The wise in heart will receive commands.
PROVERBS 10:8

To "receive" is active. There is nothing passive about God's commands. They are issued in order that we might do them.

No general in an army issues commands to his troops just to hear the sound of his own voice. He gives commands because he expects his troops to take action, to follow through, to fulfill a mission. The same is true for the Captain of our souls!

The number one reason to read your Bible is not to say you have read it. . . . The reason to read your Bible is to get your marching orders for the day and for the whole of your life.

A LOYAL FRIEND

He who loves God must love his brother also.
1 JOHN 4:21

The way you feel toward another person is not an automatic consequence of what that person did—it is a matter of what you have allowed yourself to feel. . . .

The truth is we all are different human beings with differing perspectives, ideals, and ideas about our world, but those differences should not cause brokenness among us. We should be able to live in peace with each other. One valuable trait that will enable people of differing values to have satisfactory friendships with each other is if they have loyalty toward each other. Loyalty allows us to disagree on certain things and yet be committed to our friendship and a long-term association.

GOD'S GOOD GIFTS

Let the beauty of the LORD our God be
upon us, and establish the work of our hands for us.
PSALM 90:17

God meets our needs and desires to give us good gifts because it is His very nature to do so. He cannot fail to give. He cannot fail to love.

God's gifts flow from His goodness. God's very nature of goodness motivates Him to give good gifts and to give them and give them and give them. There is no end to either God's desire to give gifts to His children or His ability to give gifts. Therefore, we can never fully exhaust the storehouse of God's gifts that are laid up for us.

TIME WITH THE WORD

For the commandment is a lamp, and the law a light.
PROVERBS 6:23

If you want to know what the Holy Spirit thinks about something, read the Bible. The Scripture is His thoughts on paper. It doesn't get any clearer than that. You and I are not left to discern the mind of the Spirit through the presence or absence of peace and the voice of conscience alone. We have His thoughts written on paper!

The most balanced Christians I know are those who spend time in God's Word on a daily basis. The most unbalanced Christians I know are those who do not. It is that simple.

WISDOM IN THE WORD

*My tongue shall speak of Your word,
for all Your commandments are righteousness.*
PSALM 119:172

God's Word says in Proverbs 6:6, "Go to the ant, you sluggard! Consider her ways and be wise." You may think, *Well, what can I learn from an ant?* I recently posed that question to a group of people, and they quickly responded:

- Cooperation
- Perseverance
- Diligence in working
- Sacrifice
- Strength in working together
- Unity of purpose

In my opinion, that's a lot to learn from one of the smallest of God's creatures!

FULL PROVISION

God is our refuge and strength, a very present help in trouble.
PSALM 46:1

God never sets up a situation or creates a circumstance without also building in the full provision, expression, or potential for success in that situation or circumstance.

God creates situations so that we might trust Him to provide for the needs, and in the process, we might grow in our relationship with Him and strengthen our ability to be and do what He has created us to be and do. Stated another way, any lack in our lives is an opportunity for us to grow in our relationship with God, and an opportunity for us to grow in our abilities and in our faith so that we can be even more effective servants of God and witnesses to God's love and grace.

GOD GOES WITH YOU

He will not allow your foot to be moved;
He who keeps you will not slumber.

PSALM 121:3

The Lord is a personal God, not limited by time or space, One who inhabits the hearts of all who believe in Him. Therefore, no temple or building can contain His presence because He is eternally present throughout the universe.

Have you ever thought that God is with you in all you do and say throughout the day? He is not just present in the morning when you awake. He is with you in the grocery store, in the doctor's office, at work, even at play. No matter where you go, God goes with you.

ACCORDING TO GOD'S WILL

If we ask anything according to His will, He hears us.
1 JOHN 5:14

Ask according to God's will—which is made clear to us in His Word. Every promise, provision, or principle of the Scriptures is for us today just as much as it was for people in Bible times.

Ask with bold confidence because of your relationship with Christ Jesus.

Ask with faith that God hears and answers all prayers for our eternal good and according to His purposes (James 1:6–7).

Ask with expectancy that God will always answer you in an exceedingly loving, direct, and timely manner.

WILLING TO FORGIVE

Freely you have received, freely give.
MATTHEW 10:8

We all are going to make mistakes from time to time and hurt others inadvertently in the process. Forgiveness is the only way to bring genuine healing to a harmed relationship so that both people can move forward in the relationship with freedom and strength.

"But," you may say, "I'm not the one at fault. Are you telling me I should still ask for forgiveness?"

Yes.

When it comes to restoration and reconciliation of a relationship, it's not a matter of who asks for forgiveness first, but rather, that forgiveness is given and received. . . . . Forgiveness surely has been received freely on our part— we must be quick to offer it freely to others.

DISAPPOINTMENT

Be doers of the word, and not hearers only, deceiving yourselves.
JAMES 1:22

Many people today get in trouble because they will not wait for either God's timing or God's method. They are so consumed with the problem of their need that they act ahead of God or instead of God. They manipulate circumstances, people, and events on their own, seeking to resolve their need according to their own timing and cunning schemes . . . which are acts of disobedience before God.

Take any sin in any place at any time, and you are going to find a great deal of manipulation at work.

The end result is never entirely good. Oh, the immediate result may seem good. But not for long. The end result will always be heavily marred by disappointment, dissatisfaction, lack of fulfillment, and diminished success.

STRENGTH AND WHOLENESS

*You were not redeemed with corruptible things,
like silver or gold . . . but with the precious blood of Christ.*
1 PETER 1:18–19

Jesus forgives you. He never holds a grudge or puts up a barrier to forgiving all your sins. He completely erases your sinful past—He alone has the full capacity to forgive and forget. . . .

Jesus never condemns you for your failures. To the contrary, when you fail, He picks you up, dusts you off, and helps you to move forward in your life. He teaches you important lessons from your mistakes so you can experience strength and wholeness.

OCTOBER

*God is bigger
than any problem.*

A WORK IN PROGRESS

Looking unto Jesus, the author and finisher of our faith.
HEBREWS 12:2

You are a work in progress. God is molding and fashioning you into a person with whom He wants to live forever.

Because of this, you have the hope that you are not going to be the same person tomorrow that you are today. If you are opening your life to God's love, and you desire to have God's love work in you and through you, then you are going to be more like Christ tomorrow than you are right now. Next week, you will be even more like Christ. Next year, you will be even more like Him. And so on. There is always more for you to *be*. There is always more inner work that the Holy Spirit desires to do.

GOOD THOUGHTS

You will keep him in perfect peace, whose mind is stayed on You.
ISAIAH 26:3

You have the ability to control what you will think. Every person has the ability to say, "I will think about something else" and then refocus the mind on a new topic, task, or problem to solve. Every person has the ability to say, "I choose to trust God," or conclude, "I choose to be overwhelmed."

Furthermore, any child of God who takes a willful stand against thoughts that clearly are harmful is going to be provided a way of escape from that circumstance. God will help you focus your mind on something other than your problem or wrong thinking if you will make the initial step.

IT WAS GOD'S BATTLE

Without Me you can do nothing.
JOHN 15:5

There were hundreds—maybe even thousands—of trained Israelite soldiers who were much more qualified to do battle with Goliath than David. But their response to Goliath's threats was paralyzing fear, stress, and frustation.

David, on the other hand, didn't seem to be upset at all. Why? Because it was God's battle, not his. Apart from the Lord, he knew he didn't stand a chance. But with the help of the Lord, he was confident that everything would turn out all right.

TALENTS AND GIFTS

*The LORD is good to all, and His
tender mercies are over all His works.*

PSALM 145:9

E ach of us has been crafted uniquely and
specifically by God for His divine plan.
To each of us, He has given talents and gifts
that are important to the accomplishment of
His purposes. No one area of giftedness is
superior to others when the talent is developed
to the highest level possible and is used for the
glory of God.

Do what God has gifted you to do with
good, consistent effort. As you work at your
skill, you will develop your skill. As you apply
your skills to help others, you will be a success
in God's eyes.

RENEWAL AND RESTORATION

*If we confess our sins, He is faithful and just to
forgive us our sins and to cleanse us from all unrighteousness.*
1 JOHN 1:9

Your salvation occurred the moment you
accept that Jesus died on the cross for your
sins. His indwelling Holy Spirit continues to
convict you of areas that need changing in your
life—habits that need to be dropped or acquired;
attitudes that need to be altered; automatic
responses that need to be transformed to line up
with God's Word and the life of Christ. You
don't need to plead with God to save you or to
forgive you or to change you. He responds to
you the moment you turn to Him to receive
His love. He then begins a renewal work that is
ongoing in you the rest of your life.

GOD IS BIGGER THAN LIFE

God is my strength and power, and He makes my way perfect.
2 SAMUEL 22:33

Long ago I came to the total assurance that God loves me, God knows where I am every second of every day, and God is bigger than any problem life's circumstances can throw at me. I have complete confidence that God is able to take care of any situation and provide an answer to any question or problem—He has all the resources of the universe to draw upon in helping each one of us through any type of crisis if we will trust Him.

He delights in showing me again and again that He is the source of my strength, my provision, my protection, and my ultimate success in life. I have absolutely no doubt that God is in control of every second of my future. Let me ask you today: Who's in control of your life?

ACCEPTED BY GOD

O LORD, You have searched me and known me.
PSALM 139:1

I am always amazed at the number of books that continue to be published . . . on the topic of self-esteem. I can only conclude that so much self-esteem material continues to be produced because many people are struggling with a poor self-image. The reason for the poor self-image is ultimately that people do not see themselves as being valuable, worthy, or acceptable to God.

When a person knows he is of extreme importance to God, and God loves him, values him, and desires to be in close relationship with him, that person has confidence and a strong self-image.

The wisdom of God leads us to see ourselves as God sees us, not as the world defines us.

SUFFICIENT IN CHRIST

When I am weak, then I am strong.
2 CORINTHIANS 12:10

Paul knew that in every area where he was weak, Christ would more than make up for his weakness, and the result would be far more strength than he could ever have apart from Christ. The same is true for you and me. When we rely on Jesus Christ to be our sufficiency, He steps in and makes us "more" than anything we could ever be in our own strength, intellect, or ability. If we are willing to trust Him and rely upon Him, He will take what we offer—doing our best and giving our best—and enhance it with His own presence, power, wisdom, and creative spirit. He will produce more than would otherwise be physically, naturally, or materially possible.

SEEK THE LORD

Those who seek the LORD shall not lack any good thing.
PSALM 34:10

What does it mean to seek the Lord? It means that we put God first in our lives. A relationship with Him becomes our priority and our foremost desire. No matter what happens to us or around us, we choose to obey God, follow God, and have a daily and intimate relationship with God. To seek the Lord means to want the Lord in your life. Those who seek the Lord are in pursuit of the Lord. They talk to Him, listen to Him, and are eager to consult Him at all times.

GOD HAS ALL POWER

*He who heeds the word wisely will
find good, and whoever trusts in the LORD, happy is he.*
PROVERBS 16:20

Where man's understanding ends, God's wisdom begins. Where man's power ends, God's power takes over. God is the One in control—not only of all things in this natural world, the political world, and the course of history and human events. He is in control of all things in the spiritual realm as well! God is the One who has all authority, power, and wisdom to set the rules, establish the process that results in forgiveness and the granting of eternal life, and give spiritual gifts to mankind.

GOD LOVES YOU

God is love, and he who abides
in love abides in God, and God in him.
1 JOHN 4:16

God does not accept us, love us, or forgive us on the basis of performance. He does not love the beautiful more than the plain. He does not love the high achiever more than the low achiever. He does not love the rich, famous, and others of high social status more than the poor, unknown, and those of low social status. Nothing you can do regarding status, performance, or appearance will elevate you one inch in God's eyes. He accepts you because you come to Him believing in Jesus Christ as the One who has taken the full consequences of your sin. He loves you because He created you and has chosen to love you from the moment He first thought of you.

ANTIDOTE FOR WORRY

*Be anxious for nothing, but in everything
by prayer and supplication, with thanksgiving, let your
requests be made known to God.*

PHILIPPIANS 4:6

The antidote for worry is a greater awareness of God's presence. When you feel anxiety rising up in you, ask God to make His presence known to you. Let Him know that you are trusting in Him. Tell Him what you would like to see happen, but add to your petition thanks for what God has done in your life in the past and praise for who God is. The more you thank and praise God, the greater calm you will experience. He is the Lord of all! All things do come from Him! He is our Provider, our Deliverer, our Savior, our Redeemer, our Rock, our Fortress, our Trust, our Life. He is the King of the universe, and He is still on His eternal throne.

MOVE ON WITH LIFE

*Forgetting those things which
are behind . . . I press toward the goal.*
PHILIPPIANS 3:13–14

There are a lot of people who live in a state
of "If Ida." If I had only done this . . . if I
had only said that . . . if I had only made that
decision. People who live in a state of regret get
stuck in the past.

Living in the past keeps a person from
fulfilling what God wants him or her to do in
the present! If that's the way you are living right
now, I heartily recommend that you ask God to
forgive you for anything you did that was sinful
or displeasing to Him in the past. After this,
forgive yourself for what you did, and move on
in your life. Choose not to dwell in the past.
Choose instead to focus on the present and to set
godly goals and make godly plans for your future.

AN INNER STRENGTH

*Those who wait on the LORD shall renew
their strength; they shall mount up with wings like eagles.*
ISAIAH 40:31

God's desire for us is that we seek Him first and foremost. Our definition for character and all matters pertaining to the human heart are to be derived from looking at Jesus and seeking to become like Him.

God's desire is that we have inner strength based upon our faith and our relationship with Him. Then when storms strike, everything around us and even our own health and well-being may take a hit, but our spirits remain vibrant, hopeful, and strong.

PREOCCUPIED WITH TRUTH

Set your mind on things above, not on things on the earth.
COLOSSIANS 3:2

Walking in the Spirit requires a mind-set, a preoccupation with truth. The battle begins not with the temptation to do something but with the temptation to dwell on anything that conflicts with what is true. This is the battle before the battle. . . .

Walking in the Spirit requires that we become hypersensitive to any thought that conflicts with truth. Anything that clashes with what is true is not of the Spirit. Anything that is not of the Spirit only gets in the way of our ability to follow the lead of the Spirit. Therefore, to walk in the Spirit, we must get serious about guarding our minds.

GOD IS THE ANSWER

Blessed is every one who
fears the LORD, who walks in His ways.
PSALM 128:1

No one person, and no one agency or system, can meet all of the needs in your life, and certainly not the deep inner needs that are vital to wholeness. A knight in shining armor who rides in to rescue the needy person and save the day so that everybody lives happily ever after is a character in a fairy tale. People can help people, but no one person can completely resolve all of the needs in another person's life. . . .

If you are looking to people to resolve all of your needs—and factoring out God—you are going to be sorely disappointed.

WE ALWAYS HAVE JESUS

Where can I flee from your presence?
PSALM 139:7

Our heavenly Father is available to us at all times. He is never too busy to hear our prayers. He is never preoccupied with other concerns to the point that He rejects our presence. Rather, He delights in having close, intimate communion with us. Whenever we are willing to spend time with Him, He is willing to spend time with us. . . .

No matter how you may feel. No matter how you may have been rejected by others. No matter how much you may hurt or how lonely you may feel, you *always* have the Lord. He is all-sufficient.

HEALING AND RESTORATION

God is the strength of my heart.
PSALM 73:26

If you go into a new relationship—personal, career-related, church-related—with the thought, I'll find love here and everything will be all right, you are likely to be disappointed. Looking to the love or appreciation of another person to solve your problem should be a giant clue to you that the problem is not one that the other's love or appreciation can solve. The problem lies within you. Something is festering deep within. And until that "something" is addressed, cleansed, healed, or restored, you will not be in a healthy position either to receive love fully or to give love generously.

Go to God and express your feelings. Ask Him to reveal the real nature of your problem and to heal you of its root cause.

THE PRODUCT OF OBEDIENCE

He stores up sound wisdom for the upright.
PROVERBS 2:7

God has provided in His Word all that we need, but we are the ones who must choose to walk "upright." To be "upright" is the result of right living; it is the product of obedience. The "upright" isn't a class of people to whom God reveals wisdom—as if we were to say that God reveals His wisdom to those who are tall, short, thin, fat, blond, brunette, and so forth. It is those who choose to obey God and who follow through and do what God commands who become the "upright."

ONE HUNDRED PERCENT

*Whoever confesses that Jesus is the
Son of God, God abides in him, and he in God.*
1 JOHN 4:15

The world tells us that we will feel secure and be free of all anxiety if we just have enough money in our bank accounts, investment portfolios, or our retirement accounts. That just isn't true. There's no lasting security in any form of financial investment. . . .

The world tells us that we will feel secure and be free of anxiety in our careers if we are promoted to positions that are high enough in the company or we achieve a certain degree of fame. That also isn't true. . . .

The truth is that the world has no magic solution for 100 percent security in any area of life. Only Jesus can give a person the confidence of security deep within.

GOD'S PROACTIVE POSITION

You are the God who does wonders;
You have declared Your strength among the peoples.
PSALM 77:14

God gives us what He knows will bring us great pleasure and joy, even though we in our finite wisdom and understanding may not know fully what we need or desire.

God does not wait for others to initiate the provision for our innermost needs. He assumes a proactive position in meeting our needs. God may use other people in the process, but He creates, orchestrates, and engineers the solution that satisfies.

WISDOM TO SURVIVE

See then that you walk circumspectly, not as fools
but as wise, redeeming the time, because the days are evil.
EPHESIANS 5:15

We live in an evil age. It's as if many organizations and institutions are out to destroy the things we as Christians hold sacred. Almost nothing in our society works to strengthen the family. No one seems to care whether married couples stay together. Just about everything on the airways teaches a philosophy of life that is diametrically opposed to what we stand for as Christians. . . .

To survive, we must be wise! We must examine everything that comes our way: every opportunity, every invitation, every relationship, everything. We must stay a safe distance away from the line separating right from wrong.

CHOOSING FRIENDS

*Listen to counsel
and receive instruction, that you may be wise.*
PROVERBS 19:20

What is the character of your close associates? Is their influence for your eternal good?

Choose your friends and associates. Don't just accept people into your life solely because they live close to you, you have known them for a long time, or you feel obligated by them to be a friend or colleague. Choose your friends and associates on the basis of their character and commitment to Christ. Choose wise, godly people. They will be a blessing to you. And through the influence of their relationship with you, you will grow in wisdom.

CLAIM GOD'S BLESSINGS

*Blessed be the God and Father of our
Lord Jesus Christ, who has blessed us with every spiritual
blessing in the heavenly places in Christ.*
EPHESIANS 1:3

I want you to notice that this verse is in the past tense. Paul did not say that God is *going* to bless us with spiritual blessings once we are in heaven, or even once we fulfill certain duties, roles, or commands. Paul wrote that Jesus Christ already *has* made all of these blessings available to us. They are blessings that are already laid up in God's storehouse for us to claim. . . .

You cannot have a need that takes God by surprise. You cannot have a need that is beyond the supply that has already been provided by your heavenly Father and made available to you by Christ Jesus!

GOD KNOWS WHAT YOU NEED

The LORD is good; His mercy is everlasting,
and His truth endures to all generations.

PSALM 100:5

Have you ever asked God for something that He did not give you? At first, you might have felt slighted or upset, but perhaps much later you saw the reason why God said no. God promises to give only what is good for you and no less. Why? The Lord loves you with an affection beyond imagination, and He fashioned every intricate fiber of your being. It makes sense, then, that He knows exactly what you need and what blessings would benefit you.

CONTENTMENT AND GRATITUDE

"I rejoice, yes, and will rejoice."
PHILIPPIANS 1:18

The apostle Paul no doubt was sorrowful and discouraged when he learned that people would preach the gospel with a wrong motive (Phil. 1:15–17). Even so, Paul refused to wallow in self-pity or engage in an argument. He chose instead to see the big picture—the result was that the gospel was being preached. He rejoiced in that! In fact, he made rejoicing a conscious decision. Paul wrote, "I rejoice, yes, and will rejoice." Regardless of how he may have felt personally, he chose to maintain an attitude of contentment, gratitude, and joy.

WORDS OF LOVE AND COMFORT

If you keep My commandments, you will abide in My love.
JOHN 15:10

There's no substitute for being in the Word daily—reading it as nourishment for your soul just as regularly as you take in food for your body. Your Bible is the number-one way God speaks to you. It is His message to you— His directives, His opinions, His advice, His words of love and comfort, His faith-building admonitions, and His commands.

Trust me on this—the Lord has a way of speaking to you as you read and meditate on the Scriptures so that you will know it is God who is speaking.

THE RESURRECTION AND LIFE

*"I am the resurrection and the life. He who
believes in Me, though he may die, he shall live."*
JOHN 11:25

Jesus declared to Mary and Martha the truth
that rings down through the generations to
us, "I *am* the resurrection and the life."
We must become aware that Jesus is with us in
the fullness of His power to be the resurrection
and the life. No matter how battered, bruised,
or even dead we may feel inside as the result of
our struggle, Jesus is with us to raise us up into
newness of life. No matter how exhausted,
broken, or devastated we may feel, Jesus is
present with us to restore us, heal us, and
energize us. He always comes to give us life and
to give us life more abundantly (John 10:10). His
very presence with us infuses life into our being.

LET GOD HANDLE IT

*Be kind to one another, tenderhearted,
forgiving one another, even as God in Christ forgave you.*
EPHESIANS 4:32

Forgiveness does not mean denying that you were hurt or that the matter was important. Rather, forgiveness means letting go and letting God. It means turning another person over to God's judgment. It means trusting God to deal with a person as God chooses, without putting yourself in the way.

It doesn't make any difference if the other person asks for forgiveness or not. Forgive. Your forgiveness should not be withheld pending the other's repentance.

Forgive quickly. The sooner you forgive, the sooner you can receive God's healing for any pain or sorrow you have experienced.

DRAW CLOSER TO GOD

The counsel of the LORD
stands forever, the plans of His heart to all generations.
PSALM 33:11

God desires to meet your needs, but His need-meeting is part of a greater process. God is always seeking to develop a closer and more intimate relationship with you. He is molding and fashioning you into the person with whom He desires to spend all eternity. He is seeking to draw you ever closer and closer to Himself.

Many of God's delays in meeting our needs are aimed at bringing us to a place where we will turn to God, trust in God, ask of God, and rely upon God. His purpose is to teach us what it means to be in fellowship with Him and to walk closely with Him day by day.

A GENUINE FRIEND

Faithful are the wounds of a friend.
PROVERBS 27:6

No two people are ever going to agree fully on everything. There must be room in a friendship for discussion and debate. There must be a feeling that the friendship is stronger than any disagreement that may arise. Genuine friends confront each other, however, in an attitude of love, helping each other to grow in Christ Jesus and to reach their maximum potential.

No person is strong all the time.

No person is correct all the time.

No person is perfect all the time.

And no person says just the right things all the time.

NOVEMBER

God's supply is precisely what we need,
the moment we need it.

CAUSE AND EFFECT

*It is appointed for men
to die once, but after this the judgment.*
HEBREWS 9:27

When you look at the whole of God's creation, has *anything* been created without a plan and purpose? The natural world provides thousands—yes, millions and perhaps billions—of examples of cause and effect, action and response, and behavior and consequence. It is only rational to conclude that God— who created everything in this universe and established all of the natural laws to govern His universe—would include a purpose for man's life that includes cause and effect, action and response, and behavior and consequence. Who we become in this life and what we do in this life are subject to divine evaluation—not only daily, but also eternally.

TURN HURT OVER TO GOD

Forgive, and you will be forgiven.
LUKE 6:37

If criticism or unkind behavior is leveled at you, you can refuse to allow ideas about these words or deeds of others to lodge in your heart. You can quickly turn to the Lord and say, "Father, help me to forgive this person. Help me to let go of this incident. I turn this person over to You to judge and deal with him. I turn this incident over to You, trusting You to resolve this in a way that results in good for me."

If you find yourself tossing and turning all night because of something you have heard or witnessed, turn to the Lord and say, "Father, wipe this from my mind and heart. Free me from this negative image or idea. Drive the enemy far from me and restore to me Your peace."

SAVIOR AND REDEEMER

*The LORD is my strength
and song, and He has become my salvation.*
PSALM 118:14

Praise God for who He is—He is our Savior, Redeemer, Victor, Healer, Deliverer, Counselor, and many other attributes found from cover to cover in the Bible.

There is no substitute for the importance of thanksgiving and praise to living in deep inner contentment.

Give thanks to the Lord daily—and often throughout the day—for all He has done and is doing for you *right now*.

YOUR JOB IS YOUR MINISTRY

*That you may walk worthy of the Lord, . . . being fruitful
in every good work and increasing in the knowledge of God.*
COLOSSIANS 1:10

We don't need more full-time Christian
workers in the church. We need more full-
time Christian workers in the marketplace with
the people who need to hear the truth. Please
don't use church work as an excuse to escape
from the ministry God has chosen for you.
Some people you rub shoulders with every day
will never darken the door of a church. You are
their only link with the truth. Humanly
speaking, you are their only hope. And that is
why God put you there. Typing reports, filing
records, selling widgets—it's all God's work.
Your attitude and excellence on the job are the
bridge to someone's heart.

WHISPER TO GOD

*I will not forget you. See, I have
inscribed you on the palms of My hands.*
ISAIAH 49:15–16

When you come to the Lord to have Him meet your needs, come to Him with a heart open to receive all that He gives you. Come with a desire to just sit for a while in the close presence of the Lord. Come with a willingness to be held tenderly in His everlasting arms. Allow yourself to relax in His presence.

If a sin comes to your mind, confess it to Him and receive His forgiveness. If a thought comes to your mind, express it to Him. If a word of praise fills your heart, voice it softly as if whispering it into His ear. . . .

This is a time for experiencing the gentle warmth of God's Holy Spirit as it flows around you, in you, and through you.

A SENSE OF COMPETENCE

Teach me to do Your will, for You are my God.
PSALM 143:10

E very person has a built-in need to feel that he is good at something. It is an "I can" and "I'm capable" attitude.

I overheard a father say to his son in a sporting goods store, "I'm not going to buy you a tennis racket. You can't play tennis." My question for that father was, "How do you know? He doesn't have a racket, so how can you know if he can play tennis?"

Never tell another person, especially a child, that he *can't* do something. It is far better to say, "Let's see what you *can* do." Set up your child for success at tasks, not failure. Give him a mind-set of trying and exploring as he discovers and develops God-given talents.

WILLING TO CHANGE

Those who dwell under his shadow
shall return; they shall . . . grow like a vine.
HOSEA 14:7

God moves us from place to place, from situation to situation, from experience to experience, to "grow us up" so He can use us more.

As long as we are willing to yield to His methods and are willing to grow and change, He will find greater and greater ways to use the talents and abilities that He gave us at our birth, as well as the spiritual gifts and potential in Christ that He gave us at our spiritual birth.

God is working and waiting and watching, always in the process of wooing His children to Himself and of preparing us to receive what He has already prepared for us.

WISDOM AND UNDERSTANDING

Get wisdom! Get understanding!
PROVERBS 4:5

The Bible declares, "Get wisdom! Get understanding!" The two are not the same. Understanding is based upon the acquisition of knowledge—it is a filtering, sifting, sorting, and defining process. Wisdom, in comparison, is an applying process.

Understanding tells us what is happening—wisdom tells us why it is happening. Understanding gives us the facts—wisdom tells us what to do with those facts. Understanding yields insight into how a problem might be solved—wisdom tells us which solution to pursue, and when and how to pursue it.

GOD PROVIDES PEACE

He himself is our peace.
EPHESIANS 2:14

God's plan was to create mankind so that we would have a relationship with Him. This relationship would be characterized by love: God's loving us and our loving Him. And through His loving presence, He would protect and provide for us.

No matter what other relationships we share, what our status is in life, where we have been and what we have done on our life journeys, God designed us to have this intimate relationship with Himself. He knew that out of this intimacy of relationship we could receive His gift to all who follow Him—a deep, lasting, abiding peace that only He can provide to the human heart.

WORKS DON'T WORK

By grace you have been saved
through faith, . . . not of works, let anyone should boast.
EPHESIANS 2:8–9

Man's works don't impress God. He responds to humility, faith, and expressions of thanksgiving and praise. God isn't impressed with what you accomplish, earn, or acquire, be it money, things, fame, or beauty. God wants a relationship with you, and in order for that relationship to be established and to grow, you must come to Him in humility and ask Him to forgive your past sin nature, to change your nature so that you will no longer desire to sin, and to help you live the life He desires for you, not the life you map out for yourself.

God wants a walking-and-talking relationship with you. Your appearance, your status before others, and your performance matter little to God. He is concerned about the state of your heart.

COMPETENT THROUGH CHRIST

My grace is sufficient for you,
for My strength is made perfect in weakness.
2 CORINTHIANS 12:9

All of us face challenges in our lives that we have never done before. Any new venture—whether it is going away to college, getting married, having a baby, starting a new job or launching a business, changing a career, embarking on an outreach ministry— will challenge your competence. If you wait until you "get it all together" before you try something you've never done before, you'll never step out to try anything. It takes faith to start something—and part of our expression of faith is our saying within ourselves, "I may be inadequate in myself . . . but with Christ dwelling in me and executing His will, plan, and purpose in me, I am adequate!"

JOY AND PEACE

The LORD has done great things for us, and we are glad.
PSALM 126:3

Can a person live in joy, peace, and contentment every second of every day throughout life? No. Moments of panic, fear, discouragement, sadness, disappointment, or pain hit all of us from time to time. But, joy, peace, and contentment can characterize the whole of your life. They can be the hallmarks of your attitude, your mood, and your outlook. . . .

When we know with certainty that God is in control, that He loves us beyond measure, and that He is at work in our lives, we have the genuine capacity to praise and thank Him even in the midst of the most dire, discouraging, or depressing times. And our praise and thanksgiving create in us very live feelings of joy and peace.

ASKING AND TRUSTING

Whatever things you ask in prayer, believing, you will receive.
MATTHEW 21:22

The purpose in bringing your needs to God is not to inform God about them. . . . He knows far more about what is going on in your life than you can ever know. . . .

So why bring needs to God in prayer to ask of Him? The main purpose is to recognize your needs. Many times as you voice your needs to the Father, you come face-to-face with your needs for the first time. God desires for you to recognize, acknowledge, and confess each need. As is true in all cases, knowing the nature of a problem is the first step toward resolving that problem.

SPIRITUAL HEALTH CARE

This Book of the Law shall not depart from
your mouth, but you shall meditate in it day and night.
JOSHUA 1:8

As you read the Bible daily, God directs you, challenges you, warns you, comforts you, and assures you. Daily reading is like preventive spiritual health care. It's better to divert a problem or to address an issue before it truly becomes a major concern. In daily reading, God refines you, bit by bit, slowly and yet continually transforming your thoughts and responses into those of Jesus.

The guidance that God gives to you in His Word is complete. It is a thorough answer. The more you read the Bible, the more you will begin to see how principles are connected and reinforced. The main themes and teachings of the Bible are repeated again and again—in different words, in different people, in different situations.

WANTING WHAT GOD WANTS

Give, and it will be given to you:
good measure, pressed down, shaken together, and running
over will be put into your bosom.
LUKE 6:38

The opposite of being self-centered is to be Christ-centered. It is to say, "What Christ wants is what I want. What pleases Christ is what I desire."

The very same is true, my friend, for your relationship with Christ Jesus. You are going to have to lay aside your personal ambitions and desires, time, material and financial resources, and energy to enter into a deep relationship with Christ Jesus. If you truly are to have fellowship with Him, you'll have a desire to open up and give of yourself—truly, give of all aspects of yourself.

UTTERLY FAITHFUL

*The LORD your God, He is God, the faithful
God who keeps covenant and mercy for a thousand
generations with those who love Him.*

DEUTERONOMY 7:9

A commitment is a pledge, a statement of a
sure promise. The value of any commitment
is based upon two things:

1. The *ability* of the promise maker to
   fulfill the promise.
2. The *integrity* of the promise maker. . . .

God certainly qualifies as One who will
stand behind His commitments on both
accounts. He has all of the wisdom, power, and
ability necessary to fulfill His promises to us. He
also has proven integrity—God has always done
what He has said He would do. God is utterly
faithful to His Word. He is holy and immutable;
He is unchanging. His character is impeccable.

BEYOND CIRCUMSTANCES

Love your enemies, bless those who
curse you, do good to those who hate you.
MATTHEW 5:44

The thing that sets the fruit of the Spirit apart from its counterpart is that the fruit of the Spirit is not environmentally sensitive. It's one thing to have peace and joy when everything is going your way. It's another thing altogether to maintain your peace and joy when the bottom falls out. It's one thing to love your children; it's another thing to love your enemy.

HEALING OLD WOUNDS

*Search me, O God, and know
my heart; try me, and know my anxieties.*
PSALM 139:23

Once we have developed an intimate relationship with the Lord, the process required for the healing of our old wounds becomes less and less painful. The most painful part of the healing process is nearly always the initial breaking of our stubborn pride, the breaking up of the crusty emotional soul of denial. . . . The more we trust Him to produce in us the nature and character of Christ Jesus, the faster and the less painful the emotional healing process becomes.

The layers of wounds are peeled from us like the layers of an onion. The layers in the soul become more and more tender, and they give way more readily to God's loving and forgiving presence.

EVERY PERFECT GIFT

*Every good gift and every perfect gift is
from above, and comes down from the Father of lights.*
JAMES 1:17

God's motives in giving to you are never
shadowy and never manipulative.
His motive is always unconditional love.
He gives you life itself. He meets your material
needs. He gives you challenges, opportunities,
and work to do. He puts you into a family and
gives you people to love and be loved by.
He redeems you from evil and calls you His own.

He gives you free will to choose to serve
Him and freedom in your spirit to be totally
yourself in His presence. He gives you the
beauty of nature. He allows you to own works
of art and to decorate your home with
possessions whose sole purpose is beauty.
Every thing you can imagine as being good
comes from God.

NEW EVERY MORNING

His compassions fail not. They are new every morning.
LAMENTATIONS 3:22–23

The One who meets our needs is fresh and new in His supply every day. He doesn't give us stale leftovers. His supply is precisely what we need in the moment we need it. Everything He gives us is fresh, new, alive, vibrant, powerful.

We cannot awaken on any given morning and be without God's mercies and His compassion. Regardless of what we have done or said the day before, God is with us in a fresh new relationship every morning.

HEALTH AND STRENGTH

Fear the LORD and depart from evil.
It will be health to your flesh, and strength to your bones.
PROVERBS 3:7–8

The person who sees his life in the context of God's plan and purpose is going to be a person who values his time and seeks to make the most of every hour God gives him.

When you value your time on earth as a servant of God, you are going to want to take care of your body. You are going to seek out God's wisdom about how to eat, how to exercise, how to get sufficient sleep, and how to engage in relaxing activities. You are going to get God's wisdom about how to defeat stress and live in contentment. You are going to fill your day with things that are fruitful and profitable. And as you put God's principles to work in your life, you are going to experience health and strength.

GOD CAN HEAL THE HURT

Pray for those who spitefully use you and persecute you.
MATTHEW 5:44

The Bible calls us to pray for the person who hurts us. Doing this draws our focus away from our hurt feelings and on to something positive and beneficial. We also are wise to ask the Lord to heal our hearts—showing us any lesson we might learn from the wounding we have experienced. We must ask the Lord to help us forgive the other person. And then, knowing that we have done all the Lord has asked of us . . . and fully expecting Him to heal us, restore us, and strengthen us . . . we must move forward with confidence and faith and His peace.

ABUNDANT BLESSINGS

*To Him who is able to do exceedingly
abundantly above all that we ask or think . . . be glory.*
EPHESIANS 3:20–21

Paul wrote to the Ephesians, God "is able to do exceedingly abundantly above all that we ask or think." In other words, you can't begin to ask God for all that He desires to give you. You can't imagine all that He has for you. I have a pretty good imagination and a pretty good boldness in asking things of God. What an awesome statement about God's supply house to think that we can't even imagine all that is contained in God's riches and that we don't have enough time on this earth to tap into all that God has made available to us!

THE GIFT OF GOD'S GRACE

By grace you have been saved through faith,
and that not of yourselves; it is the gift of God.
EPHESIANS 2:8

Your relationship with God is based upon what Jesus has done, not what you have done, do now, or will do. It's solely based upon what Jesus did on the cross. You may make mistakes, but Jesus does not. You may be imperfect, but He is perfect. God's forgiveness is based upon His plan that has been fulfilled through Christ Jesus. . . .

Receive His gift with your faith. Be assured that you have been saved and are in right relationship with Him.

STEP BY STEP

He leads me in the paths of righteousness for His name's sake.
PSALM 23:3

Moses may have thought God was calling him to fail. From a human perspective, it isn't wise for a person who has run from legal prosecution to return to the leader of the land with a stick in his hand and declare, "Let God's people go." . . .

At no time did God reveal to Moses all that he would face in his obedience, but at all times God said to Moses, "I am with you. I am leading you to the place I have prepared for you and for My people."

That same promise of God is ours. God promises to be with us always. He promises to lead us to the place He has prepared for us. Our part is to trust Him step-by-step.

WISDOM AND COURAGE

Let Your lovingkindness and Your truth continually preserve me.
PSALM 40:11

Many of our self-created needs arise because of unwise decisions. The need will be met, in part, by our making wise decisions and having the courage, skill, and determination to follow through on them. . . .

Consider the man who is neglectful of his wife. Perhaps he spends fifteen hours a day at the office and gives his wife no priority when it comes to scheduling his weekend hours. What is the solution for the need? A big part of it is likely to be a reprioritizing of plans and schedules so that the man can spend more time with his wife. Who is responsible for meeting the need? The man. What is God's role? I believe God will give the man wisdom about *how* to reprioritize his time and efforts, and will help heal the heart of the wife and make her more open to a full reconciliation with her husband.

REST IN GOD

I have learned in whatever state I am, to be content.
PHILIPPIANS 4:11

God is in control. When a job is terminated, a mate quits, a friend deserts, God is quietly but sovereignly at work for your good. You are not a victim of the economy or another's decision.

You can be content in any circumstance when you are sure of God's unceasing care and absolute control over every detail. Rest in His ability, and contentment will follow.

THE PROMISES OF GOD

Faith comes by hearing, and hearing by the word of God.
ROMANS 10:17

When a crisis strikes, remember the promises found in God's Word. If you don't know what those promises are, start today to read your Bible and underline or highlight verses, or make a list of verses in the back of your Bible so that in any crisis, you can turn quickly to God's promises. It is His desire to be present with you, provide for you, preserve and protect you, and turn all things to your good.

Memorize the Word of God, especially those passages that speak special comfort and hope to your heart. Don't wait for a crisis to hit. Have a storage bank of Bible verses lodged in your memory so that when a crisis strikes, the Holy Spirit can move your mind immediately to God's Word even if you don't have a Bible with you.

WILLING TO FORGIVE

Be merciful, just as your Father also is merciful.
LUKE 6:36

We do not have the right as Christians to harbor unforgiveness.

I have heard people say on occasion, "Well, there are some things that just can't be forgiven." Like what? What is it that Jesus couldn't forgive in your life? What is it that Jesus says is beyond His ability to cleanse, heal, restore, or forgive in a person? Take another look at your own past. If God has forgiven you . . . He expects you to be able to forgive yourself. If God has forgiven you . . . He expects you to extend that forgiveness to others.

DIRECTION FOR DECISIONS

David inquired of the LORD, saying, "Shall I pursue this troop?"
1 SAMUEL 30:8

David was totally reliant upon God for direction, not only about *what* he should do, but *how* he should proceed and *when* he should take action. He did not make the error of presuming that just because God had helped him defeat an enemy one time in one location, God would desire him to fight and defeat that enemy again in another time or another location. To knock on the door of God's plan for our lives is to recognize that God expects us always to be knocking, always inquiring, always trusting Him for daily guidance and for direction in every decision.

DECEMBER

God has a plan to bless you.

JESUS IS LORD

He who is mighty has done
great things for me, and holy is His name.
LUKE 1:49

We must never forget that when we celebrate Christ and His birth, we are celebrating the God of heaven and earth.

Some may not submit to His lordship, but that doesn't change the position the Father has given His Son. Jesus is Lord whether recognized or not, and He wants to be Lord of your life.

This is the divine structure God has ordained. . . . Anytime we fail to give Christ His rightful place in our lives—first place—we can miss out on the blessings of God.

OUR LOVING FATHER

*Holy Father, keep through
Your name those whom You have given Me.*
JOHN 17:11

Our first response when anxiety hits should be to look heavenward and cry, "Father!"

Jesus went frequently to the Father in prayer. We read in the Gospel accounts how Jesus left His disciples to be alone with God, often praying early in the morning before dawn (Mark 1:35).

Prayer shifts your focus away from the problem to the One who can give you the answer, solution, or next step to take. Prayer takes your focus off yourself—and your pain and confusion—to the Father, who knows all, controls all, has all power, and is all-loving.

KNOWING WE KNOW

Serve the LORD with fear, and rejoice with trembling.
PSALM 2:11

Obedience to His conditions is part of having a loving relationship with God. Obedience is evidence that we are trusting God to be the source of our lives. He wants to be the One on whom we depend for provision, the One to whom we look for wise counsel, the One on whom we rely for protection.

Obedience in fulfilling God's conditions is also related to our growth and development as Christian believers. We've all heard the old song that says, "I know that you know that I know that you know . . ." That's what happens when we obey. We know we are obeying, and our obedience creates in us a greater strength to ask for what we desire and to act more quickly when God directs us.

A SPIRITUAL INHERITANCE

*Giving thanks to the Father who has qualified us
to be partakers of the inheritance of the saints in the light.*
COLOSSIANS 1:12

M any of our homes are filled with precious
treasures that were passed down to us
from previous generations. Because we have
families, we share their legacy in the values and
the wisdom they have tired to teach us and even
in the material goods they have left behind.

The same concept of a rich spiritual
inheritance is repeated throughout Scripture.
The singular, wonderful thought expressed is
this: all that belongs to Jesus Christ belongs to
His saints. . . .

The believer's inheritance includes the
unconditional love of God, forgiveness of sins,
the presence of God in this world, and the riches
of eternal life in the age to come. Can any earthly
inheritance compare?

ENCOURAGING OTHERS

*He who believes in Me, the works that I do
he will do also; and greater works than these he will do,
because I go to My Father.*

JOHN 14:12

Be an encourager of the gifts of others. There is plenty of opportunity for every person to become excellent in his use of his gifts. . . .

Many people I know have a strong desire to be better than others, and they resent those who are equally talented or who seem to have superior talent. They are jealous of people who do more or better work than they do. Jesus didn't suffer from that complex. He wanted His disciples to accomplish even greater things than He had accomplished in His three years of active ministry.

THE SOVEREIGN LORD

He who dwells in the secret place of the Most High
shall abide under the shadow of the Almighty.
PSALM 91:1

God is your protector. He is the One who preserves your life from hour to hour, day to day, year to year. He is in charge of keeping you alive on this earth until the split second that He desires for you to be in eternity with Him. No matter what happens to you, God has a plan to bless you on this earth and reward you in eternity. Everything you experience, even those things that you might label "bad," God can and will turn to eternal good if you will only trust Him to be your sovereign Lord.

GOD GIVES THE GIFT

While we were still sinners, Christ died for us.
ROMANS 5:8

Only in Christianity has God reached all the way down to man and said, in effect, "All that I require of you is that you believe in My Son, Jesus Christ, and you shall have the gift of eternal life" (John 3:16).

Only in Christianity has God said, "I'll do all the work—all the dying, sacrifice, ritual, saving, regenerating, renewing—and all that I ask is that you receive what I have done and what I offer to you as being personally applicable to your own life."

PERFECTION NOT REQUIRED

*I will be merciful to their unrighteousness,
and their sins . . . I will remember no more.*
HEBREWS 8:12

Perfect performance isn't possible in this life.
God most certainly does not require it.
When self-worth is based upon performance,
anxiety and frustration are nearly always present.

Sooner or later, we all fall short of our own
best. We all come in second, third, or even last
place. We all have moments when we don't
achieve to the level we would like to achieve,
when we fail to prepare as thoroughly as we
could, or when we don't perform as well as we
have at other times. That's part of being human.
God does not require perfect performance from
us at all times, and we are unwise to require it
of ourselves or our children.

GOD'S PEACE

*Your Redeemer is the Holy One
of Israel; He is called the God of the whole earth.*
ISAIAH 54:5

At the time of Jesus' birth, there was a tremendous unrest in the world. Peace and security were the things people longed to obtain. Even though Rome had instituted its "Pax Romana," or Roman peace, there still was an unsettling lack of peace within the hearts and minds of mankind.

World peace, accumulated wealth, or material gain is no substitute for God's presence. The fact remains. Mankind needs a Savior. The birth of Jesus Christ proclaims once and for all God's infinite love to a dying world.

THE WAY YOU THINK

As he thinks in his heart, so is he.
PROVERBS 23:7

What you think makes a huge difference in what you say and do. Your thoughts, which flow out of your basic beliefs, are like the traffic controllers of your life. They determine where you go, what activities you pursue, how you pursue them, the people you are willing to include in your life, and many other factors, all of which result in your ultimate success or failure.

The way you think about other people also becomes the way you treat other people. The way you think about situations becomes the way you respond to them.

GIVE LOVE AWAY

You shall love your neighbor as yourself.
MATTHEW 22:39

You cannot love others unless you have a love for yourself that is rooted in God's love for you. A proper, healthy love for one's self leads a person to be generous and giving toward others. The person who walks wisely knows that God has loved him even though he did nothing to deserve that love, and therefore, he is much more likely to reach out with love to others even though they may have done nothing to deserve his love.

TELL GOD

*Now this is the confidence that we have in Him,
that if we ask anything according to His will, He hears us.*

1 JOHN 5:14

God wants us to ask Him to meet *all* of
our needs.

We can ask God for all needs, including those
that relate to the natural world.

We must always ask in faith and in the
name of Jesus.

We are to ask for things according to
God's will.

God will respond to our need not in a way
that is contrary to His commandments, but in
a way that is pleasing to Him and brings
Him glory.

LOVE OVERFLOWING

Love suffers long and is kind.
1 CORINTHIANS 13:4

Loving is always expressed by giving. Not all gifts are given with love, but all genuine love results in a spontaneous flow of giving—giving in words, in deeds, in objects, in other signs of affection. Love allows you to look beyond a person's actions and find a godly way to give to that person.

At times, the greatest act of love may be a gift of forgiveness, or it may be godly advice or admonition. . . . A loving heart always looks toward the highest and greatest expression of God's love in a relationship. It is love that is unconditional and overflowing.

A PROMISE FULFILLED

She will bring forth a Son, and you shall call his name JESUS, for He will save His people from their sins.
MATTHEW 1:21

How blessed we are that Jesus came! The prophets longed for His coming, but God chose us to be the ones to receive the gift of His presence. No longer is His life mere words recorded on sheets of papyrus. Instead, He is a living, breathing reality.

Have you accepted God's eternal gift of hope by placing your trust in the unchanging, unshifting reality of Jesus Christ? His birth is an anchor to the soul and a promise fulfilled that you can firmly trust.

BLESS YOUR ENEMY

Pray for those who spitefully use you. . . .
If you love those who love you, what reward have you?
MATTHEW 5:44, 46

It is easy for most of us to extend love to those we like or those who are close to us. However, Jesus taught here, as well as in other places, that our neighbor is not only the person who attends church with us, lives in our neighborhood, or is a person who is like us, but our neighbor is every person who crosses our path. . . .

And how are we to express love for our neighbors, those who are enemies as well as those who are friends or family members? We are to bless them, do good to them, and pray for them.

TURNING THE TIDE

Casting all your care upon Him, for He cares for you.
1 Peter 5:7

Anytime you have a need, problem, difficult question, doubt, or lack of substance in your life, you can turn to God immediately, make your request known, and receive His wisdom and His provision.

God's provision for you may come about in stages or steps. You may not receive immediately all that you request from Him, but the tide is turned the moment you turn to Him. Whenever you cast all of your care and concern upon Him and rely upon Him totally to supply your need and to show you how you are to live, He is quick to respond.

GOD KNOWS BEST

The LORD is good to those
who wait for Him, to the soul who seeks Him.
LAMENTATIONS 3:25

You can trust God to meet your needs with a provision that is fresh and good—it will be exciting and life-giving, satisfying and sufficient. . . .

All that God has for us is good. His supply is not only ample, but it is of the highest and finest quality.

God sees the whole of our lives, beginning to ending and on into eternity. He knows what is the best for us not only now but tomorrow and next month and next year and twenty years from now. His gifts to us are always good for us.

A PURE HEART

Have salt in yourselves, and have peace with one another.
MARK 9:50

This verse is a direct reference to purity. In Bible times, salt was the purest substance known to man. It came from the purest sources—the sea and the sun. A pure heart results in your wanting only what God wants, which is all things that are of eternal benefit. In other words, you want others around you to follow Jesus, grow spiritually, be transformed, and be blessed in all ways. Those with a pure heart desire what God desires more than what they personally want.

GOD WITH US

They shall call His
name Immanuel, which is translated, "God with us."
MATTHEW 1:23

One of the most comforting names given to
our Savior is Immanuel—God with us.
Because of the indwelling Christ, believers are
never separated from His permanent presence.
We are in Christ and He is in us. What
an encouragement! What a comfort! What an
assurance! We always have a shoulder to lean
on—the broad shoulders of Immanuel.
We always have someone to listen to our
heartache—our constant Companion and
Friend, Jesus.

INSTANT ACCESS

Because You have been my help,
therefore in the shadow of Your wings I will rejoice.
PSALM 63:7

There is no time in our lives when we are cut off from God, and therefore, there is no time when we are cut off from His supply.

You can be standing at your kitchen sink washing dishes.

You can be sitting at your desk shuffling papers.

One of the greatest privileges of your life is that you have instant access to God. You do not need to complete a certain protocol, accomplish a list of prerequisites, or be in a certain place, holding your hands in a specific way or reciting a particular statement. You can get in touch with God instantly, directly, and personally at any time of day or night, in any situation or circumstance, either verbally or silently.

OUR BEST FRIEND

No longer do I call you servants, . . .
but I have called you friends.
JOHN 15:15

All who call Jesus Savior and Lord are invited to be His friend.

What kind of friend is Jesus? He is the *best* friend you will ever have. He does for us what no one else can do, He helps us in ways no one else can help us, and He loves us as no one else can ever love us.

We may have difficulty seeing Jesus as our Friend, but Jesus doesn't have any difficulty seeing us that way.

CONTENTMENT

I have learned in whatever state I am, to be content: I know how to be abased, and I know how to abound.

PHILIPPIANS 4:11–12

Paul said that he learned to be content regardless of his circumstances—in whatever state he was in. Paul was not content *with* troubles, trials, suffering, pain, or need. He felt pain and need just as much as any other person. But he learned to be content *in* times of difficulty. His internal state was one of contentment even when his outward state was one of turmoil, trial, or trouble. . . .

His contentment was in Christ—not in things or in circumstances. His contentment lay in his relationship with the Need Meeter, not in the fact that his needs were met momentarily.

CHRIST THE LORD

There is born to you this day in the
city of David a Savior, who is Christ the Lord.
LUKE 2:11

When the shepherds found the baby wrapped in swaddling clothes and lying in a manger, they found "a Savior who is Christ the Lord." He came as a sin offering for mankind. He came as the Savior, the fulfillment of the Old Testament prophecies as the Messiah; but He came as Lord of heaven and earth also. . . .

Jesus Christ is the ruling, reigning, sovereign Lord over all.

TRULY TRUSTING

All that is in the world . . . is not of the Father
but is of the world. And the world is passing away.
1 JOHN 2:16–17

The Scriptures contain multiple references to God as a jealous God. That is, God does not desire for any person or anything—including any career, any goal, any dream—to be raised to a higher position in our lives. God wants to be Number One. He wants us to look to Him first and foremost for all of our provision, security, and well-being. He wants us to look to Him always as *the* Source of our total supply. When we experience lack, want, or need, He wants to be the first One to whom we turn for counsel, comfort, and solutions.

GLORY TO GOD!

Glory to God in the highest,
and on earth peace, goodwill toward men!
LUKE 2:14

Think of how many angels there must be—
the sky was filled with a great shining
multitude that Bethlehem night when the
shepherds gazed at the sky in wonder.
That heavenly concert was merely a glimpse
of the vast and brilliant service of worship that
continues for all time. May you join the angels
this season and always in their great cry of
praise: "Glory to God in the highest!"

ABIDING IN GOD'S LOVE

*I . . . appointed you that you should go
and bear fruit, and that your fruit should remain.*
JOHN 15:16

Jesus reveals to us things that we can never know any other way, and He enables us to do things we could never do by any other source of power. Jesus teaches us not only God's commandments and how to apply them on this earth, but He empowers us to keep and to do God's commandments. He said to His disciples: "I . . . appointed you that you should go and bear fruit, and that your fruit should remain, that whatever you ask the Father in My name He may give you."

On what basis do we bear eternal fruit? On the basis of keeping His commandments and by loving one another as we abide in His love.

ASK, SEEK, AND KNOCK

Ask, and it will be given to you; seek,
and you will find; knock, and it will be opened to you.
MATTHEW 7:7

Here in one simple and clear statement is the action God desires you to take when you perceive a need.

When you have a need, you are to ask God to meet it.

When you have a problem you can't solve or resolve, you are to seek God until He reveals the action you are to take.

When you feel shut off from the supply that you need, you are to keep pressing on in the Lord until you receive what you need for your wholeness.

NEW EVERY MORNING

*His compassions fail not. They are
new every morning; great is Your faithfulness.*
LAMENTATIONS 3:22–23

Jesus extends His love and concern to us in spite of our failure to respond. He gives and gives and gives. No matter how much we serve God, praise God, love God, engage in ministry efforts for God, we will never come close to repaying Him for all He has done for us. We will never be on an equal footing with Jesus when it comes to initiating acts of love, mercy, forgiveness, and grace.

Accept that truth. Praise God for always taking the initiative toward you. Praise God that His mercies to you are new every morning—He is continually extending Himself to you and seeking ways in which to bless you, guide you, and encourage you.

RESPONDING, NOT REACTING

*In Your hand is power and might; in Your
hand it is to make great and to give strength to all.*
1 CHRONICLES 29:12

God calls us to *respond* to life, not merely react to it. Certainly we may react in the initial moment or two of a negative circumstance or crisis. But very quickly, we must speak to our minds, *Don't panic. God is in control!* If you have gone immediately to the Father and cried out to Him for help, adding your proclamations of thanksgiving and praise, and you have done this with faith, then immediately you must follow that time of prayer, praise, and thanksgiving by saying to your mind and heart, *Believe! Trust!*

A FAITHFUL FRIEND

He will not allow your foot
to be moved; He who keeps you will not slumber.
PSALM 121:3

Jesus is utterly faithful. Whatever He says He will do, He does. You can count on His promises. His commitment to you is lasting. All that Jesus is, He will always be. His friendship never changes.

Jesus will be with us for all eternity. He has built us a heavenly home and will live with us forever.

Oh, what a Friend we have in Jesus!

EMPOWERED BY THE SPIRIT

*He saved us, through the washing
of regeneration and renewing of the Holy Spirit, whom He
poured out on us abundantly.*

TITUS 3:5–6

God is looking for imperfect men and women who have learned to walk in moment-by-moment dependence on the Holy Spirit. Christians who have come to terms with their inadequacies, fears, and failures. Believers who have become discontent with "surviving" and have taken time to investigate everything God has to offer in this life.

God's method for reaching this generation, and every generation, is not preachers and sermons. It is Christians whose lifestyles are empowered and directed by the Holy Spirit.